For Healing and Deliverance

Storming
Heaven
— with —
Prayer

ARDITH BLUMENTHAL

WESTBOW
PRESS®
A DIVISION OF THOMAS NELSON
& ZONDERVAN

WestBow Press books may be ordered through booksellers or by contacting:

WestBow Press
A Division of Thomas Nelson & Zondervan
1663 Liberty Drive
Bloomington, IN 47403
www.westbowpress.com
1 (866) 928-1240

Because of the dynamic nature of the Internet, any web addresses or links contained in this book may have changed since publication and may no longer be valid. The views expressed in this work are solely those of the author and do not necessarily reflect the views of the publisher, and the publisher hereby disclaims any responsibility for them.

Any people depicted in stock imagery provided by Getty Images are models, and such images are being used for illustrative purposes only.
Certain stock imagery © Getty Images.

ISBN: 978-1-9736-8367-4 (sc)
ISBN: 978-1-9736-8369-8 (hc)
ISBN: 978-1-9736-8368-1 (e)

Library of Congress Control Number: 2020900748

Print information available on the last page.

WestBow Press rev. date: 01/28/2020

Dedication

This book is dedicated to my husband and best friend. Thank you so very much for all the hours drinking cappuccino with me while thinking, discussing, agreeing and disagreeing regarding God's Word and His most intimate desires for our lives; and to my prayer partners, Gary and Gilda who have demonstrated their love and passion for Jesus throughout all these years. This is an effort we have all taken together, and without the years of prayers we've prayed, this book would not be written.

*By faith these people overthrew kingdoms, ruled with justice, and **received what God had promised them.** (Emphasis added). They shut the mouths of lions, quenched the flames of fire, and escaped death by the edge of the sword. Their weakness was turned to strength. They became strong in battle and put whole armies to flight. -Hebrews 11:33-24 (New Living Translation)*

Contents

Preface

A friend of mine was suffering with a debilitating set of health issues, issues she'd had for almost two decades. She had severe migraine type headaches. These were the kind of headaches that rupture the blood vessels in your eyes or make you see double. These were headaches which came about in response to brain surgery. Prior to surgery she had been diagnosed with Menièrs Disease, an inner ear imbalance that is both rare and difficult to diagnose and treat. It causes dizziness, falling, nausea and lots of other dangerous symptoms. Following her surgery she developed severe migraines which they believed had been occasioned by the nerve which the surgeons had relocated slightly to relieve the Menièrs. They also put some screws inside her skull to close the surgical site. Eventually her ailment expanded from the occipital nerve to include the trigeminal nerve as well. This affected eye movement and focus as well as her facial muscles. The pain was excruciating and kept her in bed in a dark room unable to tolerate the activities of daily living.

As sometimes happens following brain injury or alterations in state of consciousness, her case was complicated by demonic torment. After what I'd witnessed my loving Father do for my husband, God knew I would have the faith to believe for my friend's healing and deliverance as well. I now had experience with a bad report. Instead of what the medical evidence said about her, instead of what the diagnosis and prognosis said, even instead of what my friend said, I believed what God said. He's real and His Word is true. You might say, I was led to write and send these prayers, but to me it felt more like a direct command. There was such a sense of urgency inside me and it felt like a life or death situation for my friend. Every morning the prayer would pour out of me.

Believing in the power of agreement as described in (Matthew 18:20 *KJV,*) I asked five faithful intercessors to read these prayers aloud along with me and agree for her healing. We were scattered across the country and in multiple time zones, but God provided the platform for us to be together anyway. I had no idea it would be the first of more than a hundred prayers over five months. Every day there was a new prayer in my spirit. They came forth from my hand as only the Holy Spirit can cause them to do. Every day I expected to be the day her healing would happen. Every day the report came back, "Keep praying, keep believing. Nothing is changing yet."

Some days she was worse. It was literal torture to hear of her condition. Still I was motivated to stand on my faith in the truth of God's Word and the faithfulness of His promises. I knew He would heal her. Forty days passed, then sixty. Why was there no answer? The reports came in. She was worse, she was longing to die, she was at the end of her rope.

We continued to pray, not even missing a day. At around ninety days she became more desperately ill. She called me, crying, and told me she was holding a gun in her lap. She was done in. All this prayer, all of our hopes for her and her hope for herself just seemed to disappear in the despair she was experiencing. She couldn't survive another minute of suffering. We *stormed heaven*, we cried out to God, we refused to believe the enemy. We stated our hope and faith to one another and a tiny shift began, then it accelerated. The devil was pushing us all to cave. He was telling us to look at the obvious. God was not going to intervene in this hopeless case. We had our answer. Stop praying, look at the evidence. Your praying is accomplishing nothing. She's worse, the answer is "no."

But, we couldn't give up, we had to press on. We were driven by her suffering. I just knew that her "Yes," her "Amen" (2 Corinthians 1:20 *AMP*). would not be denied. God is just, filled with loving-kindness and mercy. There was no way He would disappoint us. So we pressed on. We began praying this assignment on January first. We did not back down when her symptoms grew worse, when desperation set in, when the demonic forces increased their activity. We held to God's promises and pressed in. On May twelfth, five months after our first prayer, she was delivered and healed.

My husband and I witnessed as her face muscles returned to normal, her eyes uncrossed and her vision came into focus. We were there as eye witnesses, along with her family, and we saw with our own eyes the demonic stronghold of illness and lies crumble. Her symptoms melted away and the demonic persecution ended. It was glorious. Today she is a valued member of my prayer team and has built a prayer team of her own. She knows what authority we are given through our relationship with Jesus (Yeshua), and she wants to show others what God can accomplish in their lives.

These persistent, relentless prayers were effective, not just for my friend but also for others who have passed them on or used them for their friends and family. It's my sincere prayer that you will be able to use them as a template for your most stubborn situations. Change the names and diagnosis to fit your prayer need and read them aloud one day at a time.

Acknowledgements

Sincere thanks to my husband who edited so scrupulously and encouraged me every day, my family who endured my absence and waited a very long time. Thanks to my partners who prayed over this project and were willing to go the distance; Gary, "the Karens", Gilda, Sherry, and Bridgett. Special thanks to Karen A. for her days of time and assistance in research and correctly referencing scripture and to Dr. Karen for her spiritual diagnoses. You are the best friends one could ever have.

Introduction

"O come let us worship and bow down, let us kneel before the Lord our Maker, for He is our God and we are the people of His pasture and the flock under His care" Today, if only you would hear His voice, do not harden your hearts" (Psalm 95:6-8 *AMP).*

You may wonder why a book about storming heaven begins with a prayer about bowing and kneeling. It's because it is from this position of humility and submission that we find our answers and win our battles. In understanding Him, we learn He won't deny us our requests. In pouring out our heart to Him, we learn He would never break our heart. Not only do we grow to understand our place in His Kingdom, we grow to understand His amazing love toward us. He is waiting and longing and expecting to answer our prayers and give us our heart's desire. We are members of His household, children of the King of Kings. We are heirs to all of His incredible promises and recipients of His matchless grace.

Like most people, I've had experience with prayers that seem to fall on deaf ears, prayers that appear for all practical purposes to go unanswered. In fact, at one point in my life, I actually told people if there was a God, He was a serious underachiever. It's amazing to me that He still loves me after such an insult. I'd lost family to devastating illnesses. I'd tried without success to ease the terrible suffering experienced by four members of my six person family. I watched them die untimely and painful deaths. In some cases it was more like seeing them tortured to death. If there was a formula to reverse suffering or to talk Jesus into showing mercy, I certainly couldn't find it. It was a very black time of my life.

That's why I'm excited to share this book. I spent years studying prayer, reading about prayer, praying prayers. For more than twenty years my life has been devoted to discovering how to pray effectively. I don't believe there is a formula, though I believe the format of The Lord's Prayer is an excellent blueprint. Daniel, David and Solomon give us beautiful prayers as well.

The endorsement I give for the prayers in this book is: they worked. It's not because of what I studied, read or wrote. It's because during the process of learning what touches the heart of God, what He wants, what pleases Him, I learned to pray His Word. Jesus is the Word.

> In the days of His flesh (Jesus offered up definite, special petitions for that which He not only wanted but needed) and supplications with strong crying and tears to Him Who was (always) able to save Him (out) from death, and He was heard because of His reverence toward God (His godly fear, His piety, in that He shrank from the horrors of separation from the bright presence of the Father (*Hebrews 5:7 AMP*).

If Jesus prayed this way, and was ALWAYS heard, then surely we too must bring these attributes to our prayers. Jesus clearly did not pray with indifference or any expectation of failure. He was passionate in his petitions and supplications. He cared so much about what He was asking that He cried, hard. He revered and respected God. He lived to please Him and feared displeasing Him. He knew what it was like to be in the Presence of God and He didn't want to be separated. This is our example of how to pray. "Then the Lord said to me, you have seen well, for I am alert and active, watching over my word to perform it" (Jeremiah 1:12 *AMP*).

Today God still looks for His Word to perform it, because He is bound by His Word. If, as it says; "The universe is propelled by His mighty Word of Power" (Hebrews 1:3 *AMP*), then it follows that if He were to break His Word the universe would collapse. His Word "is forever established in heaven" (Psalm 119:89 *KJV*). He is the promise keeper we have all been searching for. He delivers on what He says. He is one hundred percent reliable and can be depended upon. All of creation, heaven and earth, life and death, resurrection and eternity are based on His Word. Can you see by this that He is, in fact, unable to break it? God isn't a mere man. He can't lie. He isn't a human being. He doesn't change His mind. "Does He speak and then not act? Does He promise and not fulfill" (Numbers 23:19 *NIV*)?

The prayers in this book are scripture based, filled with urgency and prayed with tears. Persistence and the power of agreement brought about the necessary components for healing. The friend for whom these prayers were written had experienced such depth of suffering, such isolation from the outside world and such devastating loss only divine intervention could change her situation. The devil created such mayhem and chaos throughout my friend's entire household. Her family members were all roped in and bound up in a belief system supporting the devil's destructive plan. Yes, they were all believers in Jesus. They attended church, believed in the power of the Holy Spirit, and prayed daily in their own home. Even so, after so long and severe a trial they were invested in the narrative of no hope, incurable, nothing more we can do. There is no peace when satan is roaring around trying to destroy people. His lies become so monumental he can weave a deceptive web from which the only escape is the name of Jesus. It's not a reach to recognize we all are easily brought around to "it must be God's will." *Jesus paid for our salvation, our healing and delivered us from guilt* (Hebrews 1:3 *KJV*). Endless suffering is not His will. We must understand and believe the Bible which says;

> "Your righteous testimonies are everlasting and Your decrees are binding to eternity; give me understanding and I shall live [give me discernment and comprehension and I shall not die]" (Psalm 119:144 *AMP*).

I thought our team would pray for seven days, or maybe a couple of weeks, but God used the assignment to show us that sometimes a single prayer is not enough, sometimes we must *storm heaven* with prayer until the miracle arrives. "Ask and keep on asking, knock and keep on knocking" (Luke 11:9 *AMP*). We learned first hand there was demonic interference to overcome; there was chronic illness and the state of mind produced by such illness. There was heavy duty witchcraft and sorcery to banish. This series of prayers was used to that end.

I didn't know at the beginning if it would take days or weeks for the prayers to be answered. I just knew I had to pray until, as they say, something happened. My friend's life, family and destiny were at stake.

These prayers have already been passed around by family, friends and prayer team members. Everyone has asked that they be put in a book. You will find they are written in the first person. In this case, to keep them personal for you and to shield the anonymity of the subject, I have used either my late Mother or late Father's names in place of the actual subjects.

Chapter One

God Has a Plan

Have you noticed how sometimes commitment to something or someone isn't enough? Have you noticed how sometimes outside help isn't enough? In fact, even at our best, we sometimes aren't enough either. We simply can't prevail. It seems we all come to the place of needing divine intervention in order to make our way through the trials and difficult patches in our lives. We are like the label of a vitamin, "not intended to diagnose, treat, cure or prevent any disease." There are situations about which we can do nothing though we may tell ourselves we can. Just like the disclaimer on a supplement, we are woefully inadequate to promise any real relief in the time of trouble. We can help, we can pray, we can hope and stay positive, but we have no magic wand to change surrounding circumstances or situations. When people take the position they don't need the help of others, or more likely they don't need God, they are kidding themselves.

We all need real help and real answers to our problems. As a matter of course we seek the doctor when we are ill, find a counselor if problems are tough enough or seek various avenues of relief if we are in financial trouble. But the Bible says "It is through God that we shall do valiantly; for He it is that shall tread down our enemies" (Psalm 108:13 *KJV*). We all know the phrase "With God all things are possible" (Matthew 19:23 *KJV*). What gets left out of that phrase is the first part of the quote from scripture. "With men, this is impossible, but with God all things are possible" (*Matthew* 19:23 *KJV*). We can't cure ourselves, much less anyone else. But, "Christ in us, the hope of glory," (Colossians 1:27 *KJV*); has given us the authority and supernatural power to bring true cures to the suffering and real hope to the hopeless.

The devil has waged war on all mankind, first on Adam and Eve, then systematically on the rest of us. No one is immune from his deceitful ways. The scripture says "Be sober, be vigilant; because your adversary the devil walks about like a roaring lion, seeking whom he may devour" (1 Peter 5:8 *KJV*). His plan includes whatever is required to destroy you completely. He came to "kill, steal and destroy and has been a liar from the beginning" (John 10:10 *KJV*). But there is very good news: We have authority over him and his plans for us if we truly believe and understand the power we have in and through Jesus. The devil may resist submitting to our authority but the Bible says he must. We may have to insist and resist and drive him away but he must obey us. *He is under our authority because we are "in Christ" and have been delegated the necessary power to rule over the enemy and all his plans for us* (Luke 10:19 *KJV*). We may have to mount a full-on assault to remove him and his demonic followers, however, *if we persist and resist, he will withdraw* (James 4:7 *KJV*).

The Old Testament is filled with conflict, intrigue and all out war. Many of God's encounters with man center on these themes.

God demonstrates over and over His ability to bring the under through the impossible situation and deliver a great victory.

Joshua, who led the children of Israel across the Jordan River into the Promised Land, was, among other things, a battle strategist and an amazing leader. Where did he get those abilities? His leadership and authority flowed out of his relationship with God. He knew beyond question that God was a promise keeper. He walked with Him, following the cloud by day and the fire by night. He and Caleb were the last of the old guard. The rest of those who came out of Egypt were dead and gone. When God told Joshua how the defenses of Jericho fortress were going to fall, Joshua didn't question God's plan. He believed Him. What warrior would believe a battle plan where one would send his men to march around a city, seven times, no less, and then blow a bunch of trumpets and give a shout? I've stood on the ruins of those old walls in Jericho. One could still use them for a highway because they are so thick and solid. But Joshua believed in God's plan for victory, executed it, and emerged with his army intact. That is what happens when we follow God's plan into the battles of our lives.

God provided Joshua a blue print, a battle plan, as He always does for our battles too. Joshua believed God's plan, no matter how outlandish it may have seemed to everyone else. For example "circumcise every male in the nation of Israel." Now there's an idea! But, guess what? Joshua did it. There were six-hundred thousand men in the camp so it was no small job. I can't help think not everyone was lining up for the chance either. Some slackers were probably dragged in. But it shows us the serious nature of preparing for battle. It costs something; sometimes it costs a great deal. Battling until there is victory is not a trifling matter. We need to be set apart and consecrated for the task at hand. In Joshua's day it was through the covenant of circumcision. In our day it is through our faith in the power of the blood of Jesus. "Faith is the victory that overcomes the world "(1 John 5:4 *KJV*).

Joshua told his men to "Prepare the provision" (Joshua 1:11 *KJV*). In other words, his men had to be ready to fight. They needed to pack up and take everything they needed along with them. Once started, there was no turning back. He wasn't planning to go into battle without the weapons, supplies, equipment, the bread or water necessary to see the troops through to the end. So often we embark on a "God mission" like it's merely a good idea. No, we need to prepare our provision too. A prayer assignment is a battle, pure and simple. Someone's life is depending on it. Make certain you have a backup plan, and have "put on the whole armor of God that you may be able to stand against the wiles of the devil" (Ephesians 6:11 *KJV*). Be prepared for the unexpected. Sometimes we can be sabotaged, severely sidetracked, interrupted or lost in the weeds. We can even end up in a wilderness of our own. Your map and compass are part of your provisions as well.

Joshua instructed his people to follow the Ark of the Covenant. The Ark was Joshua's map and compass. The Ark was being lifted up by the priests of Israel as they led the way. The reason: "You've not passed this way before" (Joshua 3:4 *KJV*). "You shall command the priests who bear the Ark of the Covenant, saying, 'When you have come to the edge of the water of the Jordan, you shall stand in the Jordan" (Joshua 3:8 *NKJV*). The people were to stop and just watch what the God of Israel was about to do. Joshua said, "Behold, the Ark of the Covenant of the

Lord of all the earth is crossing over ahead of you, (leading the way) into the Jordan" (Joshua 6:3, 8 *AMP*). So too, we follow the Holy Spirit as we take new spiritual territory. There is no point in going unless the Holy Spirit is leading the way.

When Joshua's men suffered a defeat at the battle of Ai, the Bible says *the hearts of the Israelites melted with fear. They were filled with doubt regarding the promises of God. The previously undefeated Israelite army fled as cowards before its enemy. Joshua fell on his face in mourning before the Lord. He tore his clothes and along with the elders of Israel, put dust on his head* (Joshua 7:6-9 *KJV*). Why? Why did God bring him this far and allow him to be defeated? God responded to Joshua with two words. "Get up!" "Why is it you are laying on your face like this" (Joshua 7:10 *NIV?*) In other words, get busy with your assignment. Stop feeling sorry for yourself. You haven't completed what you committed to do. You have an empire to start, a land to conquer, a sick person to heal, someone in bondage you need to deliver. Start again. Consecrate again. Set yourselves apart from your failure and proceed with God's plan. Setbacks and obstacles are part of satan's plan (here and elsewhere, satan is not capitalized as he doesn't merit that recognition). He is the one who is trying to take the wind out of your sails. God is telling you; get up, start again, go forward. Don't show satan any mercy, this is your victory so move on.

"Have I not commanded you? Be strong and courageous! Do not be dismayed for the Lord your God is with you wherever you go" (Joshua 1:9 *KJV*).

Because of the shed blood, death and resurrection of Jesus we know beyond a shadow of doubt our victory over the forces of darkness is inevitable. Like Joshua, all we need for our victory is God's battle plan, and our own fierce resolve to follow it through emboldened by His strength and courage. Sometimes it takes an army to storm the stronghold until the wall falls down, but God has provided a map and compass for us to take down the walls of the Jericho in our own lives.

"Does not My word burn like fire?" says the Lord "is it not like a mighty hammer that smashes a rock to pieces" (Jeremiah 23:29 *KJV?*)

Fortunately, we don't generally have to fight for earthly territory or take over another kingdom as Joshua did. We have the military to do that on our behalf. However, as ambassadors in the Kingdom of Jesus, (whose name in Hebrew is Yeshua,) our battles are "against, powers, principalities, evil rulers of this age, and wicked spirits in heavenly places" (Ephesians 6:12 *KJV*). We are meant to battle evil in all its forms, but also to love, exhort and help one another. Remember, as His ambassador, you are a diplomat. You represent His Kingdom and His principles. You need to use the policies of heaven in order to create the atmosphere for "Thy Kingdom come, Thy will be done, on earth as it is in heaven" (Matthew 6:10 *KJV*).

The earthly ministry of Jesus, our King, brought us the good news of the gospel; fulfilled the prophecy of Messiah Redeemer, and demonstrated the kindness of comforting the mourner, caring for the orphan, feeding the hungry, healing the sick, driving out demons and raising the dead. He told us outright his followers would have the authority to do the same. He told us outright if we prayed in His name, believing, we would receive what we asked for. Jesus, Yeshua, changed the world, sat down at the right hand of God, and left us with the ability to change the world too.

Chapter Two
God Will Do It

Part of my prayer training came recently when my husband was diagnosed with Stage III colon cancer. His baseball sized tumor was attached to both the small and large intestines, his abdominal wall, and his bladder. I was told it was too late for him. His course of therapy included ten chemo treatments and a ten-plus hour surgery to remove the tumor. He was very ill by the time he was diagnosed, having lost fifty pounds and a lot of blood, giving him high risk blood counts and very low iron. I called everyone I knew who prayed even a little and everyone agreed to pray for him. Though his condition was poor and his cancer advanced, miracles started happening right away. I tell him that God put him on a satin pillow and carried him through the entire process. First, we had the best doctors in the best facilities. It was as if prayer lifted him above all his symptoms, including adverse side effects from chemo-therapy, or post surgical pain. He gained weight on chemo, had no adverse side effects, didn't need a colostomy, recovered from his surgery weeks ahead of predictions, and never needed a single pain pill. He is the poster boy for how to be sick without getting sick. I asked his physicians if others had a similar response to so many chemo treatments. They told me they didn't know because no previous patient had been able to tolerate more than five such treatments! Now his recovery is complete and he is cancer free. He's happy and healthy, recovered as if he had never been sick. But this prayer book isn't about him exactly.

I did learn some valuable lessons about prayer from his journey though, and I want to share a few of them before we begin.

1. *God is hampered in His Work when we stand in the way. Surrender means just that: surrender. The minute we take the problem or challenge into our own hands we force God to step back. When we ask Him to fix something we then must allow it.*

If you've ever intersected with the US health care system you know it can be both time consuming and overwhelming. Thrown in among insurance, government, doctors, test facilities and hospitals one can be easily confused, frustrated, derailed or discouraged. Because I was a nurse, I even know the jargon, and have no fear of the "medical or insurance authorities." Even so, it was daunting and profoundly frustrating just to get the necessary approvals, locate a treating physician and schedule within an approved network. In two and a half days of trying to set up my husband's care I actually spent fourteen hours on hold! I was literally at my wit's end. It was then, in tears of frustration, I wept before the Lord. It was all clearly beyond my capability and control. My husband had cancer. He was dying before my eyes and I couldn't fix it. After three days of my best efforts I seemed completely unable to find anyone who could help me find the care he needed. One hospital, specializing in cancer, said they would under no circumstance deal with our insurance plan and hung up on me.

I told God I was at the end of my ability and asked Him to take care of my husband. He graciously saw my desperation and picked him and me off the floor and went to work on our behalf. It was not a, "let's see what you can do God," kind of surrender. I said, "Whatever You want to do God, my husband belongs to You. This is beyond my ability." I was fully aware I had just given God permission to end my husband's life if that was what He decided to do. In fact it was permission for Him to take complete control. If I was going to put my trust in God's abilities, promises and plan then I had to end the practice of trying to second guess any part of what God had in store for us. Within a few hours of turning it over to God I received a call informing me the best doctor in New York City for treating this particular cancer was available and would take his case. Furthermore, the "no, not covered by this insurance policy," I received from the doctor and hospital was completely reversed. They said "We didn't know we had a contract with your insurer and we don't remember having one, but it seems we do and you are covered." It was the first of many miracles.

2. *If You want God to focus on your request, you must focus on Him. Worship Him. Praise Him. Thank Him. Remember, you can't fix it, so you have plenty of time to spend in His presence.*

As a wife and friend to my husband I knew both of us would need prayer support. I couldn't serve as his minister or his health care provider. Those things I'd given to God. But I did solicit help from reliable prayer partners and asked them to pray each day for us. I knew I was too close to the situation and would try to micromanage God as well as the doctors and nurses. When I surrendered to God's plan for us, whatever that might be, I no longer needed to manage the medical staff or schedule. His care was off limits for me and rightly so. My God has no limits and He was managing everything. He was delivering us in a way that was far beyond our wildest dreams. All I had to do was "Stand firm and see the deliverance of the Lord" (2 Chronicles 20:17 *KJV*).

3. *There is power in praying in agreement with others. God designed it that way. Build a prayer team now, before the storm.*

For years I prayed often and with mixed results. It was never a matter of faith, I believed God would heal, but I did want *my* desired result. I now believe God wants us to trust in *His* desired result. His plan will be for our good, not our harm. Because He lives outside of time, He already knows exactly what needs to happen in any situation.

4. *God wants you to see Him and His great love for you. Guilt is a barrier between you and God. Don't blame the sick person and don't blame yourself.*

I knew a long time before my husband received his diagnosis something was really wrong with him. He'd lost fifty pounds and looked like a ghost. He fell asleep whenever he sat down for two minutes. I didn't push him hard enough to get him to the doctor. I had plenty to feel guilty about and so did he. But guilt interferes with the task at hand. It holds us back and hampers our prayer life and our growth. Set it aside. You are completely forgiven and accepted as a member of God's household. "When He had accomplished our forgiveness of sins and riddance of guilt, He sat down" (Hebrews 1:3 *AMP*).

5. *Your personal peace is a direct measurement of your trust in God. When you fully trust Him, you can rest assured He is taking care of everything, so worry is unnecessary.*

Surrender does not mean you stop praying, speaking God's Word over your situation, or fighting for yourself or your loved one. It does, however, turn off the worry and fear. The devil doesn't retire when you surrender to God. In many cases he'll step up his game in order to get you to take your concerns back on your own shoulders. True surrender results in true peace. God is the complete answer. Whether He heals, cures, or takes a loved one home to be with Him, He knows your story and how to work everything together for your good.

6. *Remember, God will use your trials and challenges for His glory.*

The day my husband came home from the hospital following his surgery the Lord told me to begin a prayer assignment for someone else. God was changing the subject! This was shocking to me but I immediately agreed to take the job. The miracle God performed for us gave me the faith to believe ALL the promises of God. I knew His healing work with my husband

and me was concluded: The healing was complete. All the rest was cake!

7. *God's character and power have been obvious since the beginning. He's waiting for us to acknowledge and follow Him.*

We may want to reserve judgment or not talk about it; we may want to nurture our doubts and continue to fear that God doesn't control the universe, down to the last atom. But, if not He, then who? One can't worship or look to one's self as the source. On second thought, I guess one could, but it's hardly worth considering. Worshiping others is always disappointing because every human turns out to be flawed or disappointing sooner or later. Objects provide no meaningful edification or interaction. A relationship with the Creator of the Universe is too wonderful to reject.

"Ah! Lord God! Behold, You have made the heavens and the earth by Your great power and by Your outstretched arm! There is nothing too difficult or too wonderful for You" (Jeremiah 32:21 *NIV*). Isn't that an incredible piece of information? It doesn't matter how the odds are stacked against us, how many rejections or "no's" we have encountered; how bleak the landscape or withered our hope. God is bigger still. *Nothing is too hard for Him (Jeremiah 32:27 KJV).*

Chapter Three

Preparing for Strategic Prayer

Important questions to ask before embarking on a prayer assignment:

1. Have you fully and freely forgiven those who have offended, betrayed or hurt you?

If we carry resentment, bitterness and judgment into our prayer assignments our prayers will not be heard.

> But if you do not forgive others their trespasses, (their reckless and willful sins, leaving them, letting them go, and giving up resentment) neither will your Father in heaven forgive you your trespasses *(*Matthew 6:16 *AMP)*.

"Above all things have intense and unfailing love for one another, for love covers a multitude of sins, forgive and disregard the offenses of others" (1 Peter 4:8 *NIV)*.

2. Do you believe you are fully and freely forgiven by God?

Jesus paid for our redemption in full, once and for all. He did that as a gift to us. We were bought back and returned to our original inheritance. His redemption includes being saved from sin, delivered from bondage and healed from disease. Grasp that. The Bible says we are "saved to the uttermost" (Hebrews 7:25 *KJV*).

When He (Himself and no other) had (by offering Himself on the cross as a sacrifice for sin) accomplished purification from sins and established our freedom from guilt, He sat down (revealing His completed work) at the right hand of the Majesty on high (revealing His Divine authority). For with the heart a person believes in Christ as Savior, resulting in his justification (that is, being made righteous being freed of guilt) (Hebrews 1:3 *AMP*).

Because of what He did for us, we have the standing to go before His throne to ask for help in our time of need.

3. Do we have the authority to heal the sick in Jesus name? Yes, the scripture clearly gives us that authority.

"I have given you power to tread serpents and scorpions underfoot, and to trample on all the power of the enemy; and in no case shall anything do you harm" (Luke 10:19 *NIV*).

Healing

I assure you and most solemnly say to you, anyone who believes in Me as Savior, will also do the things that I do; and he will do even greater things than these (In extent and outreach) because I am going to the Father. And I will do whatever you ask in My name (as My representative) this I will do so that the Father may be glorified and celebrated in the Son. If you ask Me anything in My name (as My representative) I will do it (John 14:12-14 *AMP*).

"I will do whatever you ask in My name so that the Father may be glorified through the Son. Yes, I will grant whatever you shall ask in My name" (John 14:13-1 *AMP*).

"By the stripes that wounded Him we are healed and made whole" (Isaiah 53 4a-5c *AMP*).

"With God all things are possible and nothing is impossible" (Matthew 10:27 *NIV*).

"Now, empowered by His Word and the Holy Spirit and expecting victory, never worry about anything. Instead, in every situation let your petitions be made known to God through prayers and requests, with thanksgiving" (Philippians 4:6 KJV).

"I assure you most solemnly I tell you, that My Father will grant you whatever you ask in My name. Ask and keep on asking and you will receive, so that your joy may be full and complete" (John 23b and 24b *AMP*).

"I am the Lord who heals all your diseases" (Exodus 15:26c *KJV*).

"O Lord my God, I cried out to You for help and You have restored my health" (Psalm 30:2 *KJV*).

"The Lord hears his people when they cry to Him for help. He rescues them from all their troubles. He is close to the brokenhearted; He rescues those who are crushed in spirit" (Psalm 34:17 *NIV*).

"This I know, God is on my side" (Psalm 56:9b *NKJV*).

"Surely He has borne our griefs (sicknesses, weaknesses, and distresses). With his stripes we are healed" (Isaiah 53:4 *AMP*).

These prayers are conversations with God about our concern over a sick friend. It is my recommendation that you adapt and read one prayer each day. When read all together they can appear repetitive though each is a unique request. They are personal; however, they can be changed easily to fit the diagnosis or person for whom you are praying. The names within belong to my late parents.

Chapter Four

Prayers One to Ten

*And whatsoever You ask in my Name,
that will I do that the Father will be
glorified in the Son~(John 14:13 KJV).*

Prayer One

Mighty God, Captain of the Hosts of Heaven's Armies, Ruler of the Universe, We come to You in the Name of Jesus, our King and Sovereign.

Thank you for making it possible for us to come boldly before You. Thank You for the amazing plan of salvation and for the redeeming grace released to us through Your Son, Jesus.

We've assembled a team to pray for Your daughter Carol, and *we are in agreement about making our requests known to you for her healing and deliverance* (Philippians 4:6 *KJV*). "Where two or more are gathered in Your name, You are in the midst" (Matthew 18:20 *KJV*). We have agreed to pray together until You answer our prayers.

Now, knowing Who You Are, *we come to You for help in our time of need and we place our requests before You* (Hebrews 4:16 *AMP*). *You have offered to hear us when we pray; and You guarantee You will honor requests made according to Your will* (1 John 5:14 *KJV*). Thank You so much for that. What a kind and loving Sovereign You are to Your people. No other god ever made a promise like that.

Today we raise our voices to thank you for the many times You have answered prayer in the past. Thank You for Your miraculous dealings in the affairs of man and specifically for Your miraculous dealings in the lives of those we love and pray for. We loose on earth what is already loosed in heaven (Matthew 16:18-19 *KJV*): healing, salvation, and deliverance. We release to her the ability to stand in the power of Your strength. We release grace and confidence because we know You are showing Yourself mighty on her behalf. We release healing by and through Yeshua, Jesus, our Salvation and Song. *He who heals by His stripes have made her whole* (Isaiah 53:5 *KJV*). We proclaim she is glowing with health. We release *"beauty for ashes, the oil of joy for mourning and the garment of praise for the spirit of heaviness"* (Isaiah 61:3 *KJV*). Thank you so much for hearing and answering our prayer. We bless Your Holy Name, now and forever. Amen.

Prayer Two

Thank You for being the Mighty God (El Shaddai) who hears and answers prayer. You are our Sovereign in all things.

We enter Your Throne Room in the co-authority granted us through Jesus, *who gave us the power over ALL the power of the enemy. The enemy can by no means harm us* (Luke 10:19 *KJV*). *We embrace our Jesus-given authority and bind (restrain, forbid) all the plans, strategies and tactics satan has devised to afflict Carol for whom we pray* (Matthew 16:19 *KJV*). We proclaim that "no weapon raised against her will succeed" (Isaiah 54:17 *AMP*). We forbid the manifestations of evil related to satan's diabolical assignment, including such things as pain, sorrow, guilt, disappointment, despair, hopelessness, fatigue and disability.

From this moment forward, we release the healing power of Yeshua, Jesus, to every nerve, fiber, synapse and muscle. We release healing to her brain, head, neck, shoulders, spine and the rest of the body. We put You in remembrance of Your Word and declare *satan must repay every second, minute, hour and day he has stolen from Carol,* (Proverbs 6:31 *KJV*). We forbid the power of curses, malicious gossip and hurtful words. We release *Your Word which says healing is Bread for Your children* (Matthew 15:22-29 *KJV*).

Please rebuke the enemy and prohibit him, his demons and dark forces from afflicting Carol any longer. We beseech You to release Your angels to minister and restore her just as they did for Jesus after he was in the wilderness for forty days. (Mark

1:14 *KJV*). Prohibit the demonic battle raging over her health and life and saturate her in Your Living Word, which is our "very life" (Deuteronomy 32:47 *AMP*). Release her from bondage and restore freedom, deliverance, and a life filled with Your peace (shalom): nothing missing, nothing broken, nothing lost.

We agree she is made completely whole in the Name of Jesus. We stand amazed at Your mercy, Your loving-kindness, Your compassion, and Your healing power. We forbid any retaliatory actions the enemy might attempt against the prayer team or Carol's family. We acknowledge Your might and power and realize no man can do what we ask, only the Spirit. Amen

Prayer Three

Wonderful Counselor, Mighty God, Everlasting Father, we are interceding on behalf of Your daughter Carol, in the Name of Jesus, Yeshua. We thank You for hearing us when we pray.

We are grateful You are "high and lifted up" (Isaiah 57:15 *KJV*). You don't see things from only our point of view. You have a lofty and eternal viewpoint and hold our best interests in Your heart. *You know how to work all things together for our good* (Romans 8:28 *KJV*). You are amazing!

> Christ cancelled and blotted out and wiped away the handwriting of the note (bond) with its legal decrees and demands which was in force and stood hostile to us. This bond, with its regulations and decrees and demands, He set aside and cleared completely out of our way by nailing it to His cross. We are no longer under the curse (Galatians 3:13 *AMP*).

"We have been raised with Christ to a new life, thus sharing His resurrection from the dead and we seek eternal treasures that are above" (2 Corinthians 5:17 *NIV*).

> Our lives are hidden with Christ in God and the Word spoken by Christ the Messiah has found a home in our hearts and dwells in us. We have been rescued and delivered from wrath and

invested with all the privileges and rewards of new life in Messiah (Romans 5:9 *NIV*).

It is those privileges and rewards we seek now on Carol's behalf.

Because of the work of Jesus, we know and trust she has been radically transformed, delivered and granted perfect health, soul harmony, and peace. She has been made whole. *She is more than a conqueror and has gained a surpassing victory over illness, disease and infirmity* (Romans 8:31-39 *AMP*). The enemy is neutralized and can no longer harm, damage or harass her in any way. Salvation through Jesus includes deliverance from all the power of the enemy. We claim and release wholeness for Your daughter. The enemy must cease and desist. We declare shalom over the entire family. *Give your angels charge over them* (Psalm 91:11-12 *KJV*).

Thank You Lord, "You are Mighty in power and abounding in compassion" (Psalm 86:15 *KJV*). Amen

Prayer Four

Abba, Thank You for Your continuing mercy and grace. Thank You for being ever true to Your Word (Psalm 19:9 KJV). Thank You for the treasure of Your Word and for the authority You have given us to change circumstances and situations through prayer.

You are so generous and kind. Thank You for Jesus, Yeshua, in whose name we pray. We've come to storm the gates of heaven on Carol's behalf! We come boldly to Your throne *knowing we are hidden in the shadow of Your wings and invisible to the enemy* (Psalm 91:4 *KJV*). *We are wrapped in the righteousness of Yeshua* (Romans 3:22 *KJV*). We restrain and forestall the enemy forces attempting to throw our mission off plan. *May these prayers rise before You as sweet incense* (Psalm 141:2 *KJV*).

We entreat You to heal Carol at this very moment. Look upon her suffering and reach out Your healing, saving hand to deliver her from all pain, all suffering and all sickness. We release her to a life worth living, a life of abundance of health, a life filled with Your joy and *a life to use according to Your plan and purpose* (Jeremiah 29:11 *AMP*).

The assignments You have given her cannot be realized from a bed of pain. We prohibit the bars of Carol's prison to contain her any longer. We break every chain the enemy has placed around her body, soul, and spirit. We bind and dismiss the devilish assignment of infirmity and we bind despair and hopelessness from her life forever. We dismiss fear, pain and suffering and forbid them from harming her further. *We restrain the powers, principalities, evil rulers of this age and wicked spirits in heavenly places from interfering with her God-given assignments* (Ephesians 6:10-12 *KJV*). We have God-given power and authority over all of them.

We set forth a shift from suffering to restoration. We set forth a shift from darkness to light. *Send Your light to expose truth* (John 1:5 *KJV*). Lord, all things are possible with You. Look upon Carol with compassion. *Reach out Your mighty right hand to heal and deliver* (Isaiah 41:10 *KJV*).

Thank You and bless Your name forever. Amen.

Prayer Five

Triune God, You are perfect in all Your ways. Nothing is too hard for You.

Today we lay everything aside to stand in the gap for Carol's manifest healing. Father, this is urgent! She is unable to defend herself against these demonic assaults without You. The pain, fatigue and disappointment are too much for her to bear.

We ask, according to Your Word, *that the Son of Righteousness, Yeshua, Jesus, arise with healing in His wings* (Malachi 4:2 *KJV*). We release from heaven, total restoration of every afflicted cell. We release from heaven, strength for today. We release from heaven, health and healing to every nerve, fiber and sinew. We release the hope and joy found only in You. Abba, we put You in remembrance of all Your promises to Carol. *You chose her before the foundation of the world and loved her before she was ever conceived* (Psalm 139:14-16 *KJV*). *You have gifted her with every spiritual blessing because this is Your kind intent* (Ephesians *1:3-4 KJV*). You welcomed her into Your family and offered her a life of abundance. We release that abundant life to her now.

We restrain and forbid want and lack and ask you to release her to green pastures by still waters. We expect her full healing and deliverance. *Anoint her head with oil in the very presence of her enemies* (Psalm 23:1-6 *KJV*). "The Lord's hand is not shortened, that it cannot save; neither his ear heavy, that it cannot hear" (Psalm 59:1 *KJV*). We know Your mercy will prevail. We release Your mercy and goodness to follow her from this moment forward.

You have given us, as Carol's intercessors, authority over all the power of the enemy (Luke 10:19 *KJV*), *and a power mighty in God for the pulling down of strongholds* (2 Corinthians 10:4 *KJV*). We therefore pull down, in the name and authority of Jesus, the stronghold of infirmity, disability, and pain and release a life of God's mercy and grace instead. We release healing and wholeness in the matchless Name of Jesus. Thank you for hearing and answering our urgent prayer. Amen.

Prayer Six

Abba, Father, in the mighty, unmatched Name of Jesus, Yeshua, we come before You.

We are deeply aware the enemy, the serpent, is taking a last stand for Carol's life.

With *the Sword of the Spirit, which is the Word of God* at the ready (Ephesians 6:17 *KJV*), we forbid the continuation of this opposition. "Greater is He in each of us, than he who is in the world" (1 John 4:4 *KJV*). These dark forces have already been taken captive by the power of the cross and the death and resurrection of Jesus. *Their power was dismantled and put to public shame* (Colossians 2:15 *KJV*). They cannot touch this anointed child of the living God. They are lying to her.

Carol has been set free by the blood of the Lamb, *Jesus, who is the resurrected and living Messiah. She is His child* (Galatians 3:36 *KJV*). We pronounce aloud the Word of truth and command the enemy to let go of his prey and retreat. We ask You to rebuke satan on Carol's behalf. We forbid his return and disallow him to send replacements. We release clear vision, sharp and incisive thinking, freedom from fatigue and freedom from pain. *You, O Sovereign Lord, have imbued us with power to command the forces of darkness and compel them to comply with Your Word* (1 Peter 5:8 *KJV*). We prohibit them from further action against the health and well-being of Your child.

Please send angelic ministers to feed and restore her (Hebrews 1:14 *KJV*). Amen.

Prayer Seven

Abba, we lay Your daughter at Your feet. Jesus, our Healer, is seated at Your right hand and He is interceding right now, (Romans 8:34 KJV).

Jesus loves Carol and has promised her all of His promises are true (2 Corinthians *1:20 KJV*). He is the One "through whom You speak in these last days. He is the exact representation and the perfect imprint of Your essence. He propels universes and all things with His Mighty Word of Power" (Hebrews 1:1-3 *AMP*). We appeal by and through Your beloved Son for Carol's complete deliverance and healing. We are not a half-way people and You are not a half-way God. "Every good and perfect gift is from above, coming down from the Father of heavenly lights who does not change like shifting shadows" (James 1:17 *NIV*).

We are following Your instructions as we release Heaven's healing for her, a complete healing. We know beyond any doubt the gates of Hell cannot prevail against Your great love and infinite mercy.

We speak with faith to the mountain of despair and hopelessness created by years of disappointment and suffering and command this mountain to be removed into the sea (Mark 11:23 *KJV*). We have more than a mustard seed of faith. We believe in You our Comforter and the Solid Rock on which we stand. *Your Word is true. Send it forth to heal and perform on Carol's behalf* (Psalm 107:20 *KJV*). Don't delay another moment, it's an emergency.

We trust in and rely on You alone. Amen.

Prayer Eight

Abba, You are still God today, yesterday and forever. You are still on Your Throne and You are still the focus of our adoration and praise.

We return to Your Throne Room. *We are not taking a break or abandoning our post until Carol is strong in Your Strength and upheld by Your Mighty Hand* (Isaiah 41:10 *KJV*). We know her healing is even more critically important to You than it is to us. *We are literally a part of the body of Christ* (1 Corinthians 12:27 *KJV*). When a member of the body is in pain, *all of the body and especially the head, who is Jesus, doesn't rest until his entire body is without spot or wrinkle and we can be presented holy and blameless* (Ephesians 5:27 *KJV*).

This has been the most puzzling of medical cases. The enemy has tried every trick to destroy Carol's health, well-being and serenity. *He has shown no mercy and has employed many illegal strategies and tactics to kill and destroy her* (John 10:10 *KJV*). *We take authority over the enemy's activities* (Luke 10:19 *KJV,*) as they relate to Carol's health and well-being and release her from the bondage brought about by illness. Please make it now; today.

Set Carol's feet in a high and large place (Psalm 18:33 *KJV,*) and bless her with every good and perfect gift. Protect and provide for the vision and calling for which she was born. May we see her destiny fulfilled in our life-time.

You are our hiding place, our fortress and high tower (Psalm 61:3 *KJV*). You are our solid rock and our anchor in tempestuous times. You surround and enclose us under the shadow of Your wings. We find our hope, our strength and our very being in You (Acts 17:28 *KJV*). "We can do nothing without You, but with You, ALL things are possible" (Matthew 19:26 *KJV*). (*Emphasis added*). Amen.

Prayer Nine

Abba Father, with gratitude and joy for Your mercy and love, we bring Carol to Your Throne Room. We are grateful beyond words for the mercy and grace You've already shown toward her. Thank You for the emergency relief You've granted! Thank You for the ransom You provided through Jesus to purchase her life.

Carol is no longer facing the enemy alone. Thank You for Your promise that she will be healed and delivered. *You are a God of action, of power and of might* (Isaiah 53:4-6 *KJV).*

Father we pray You will continue this good work You have begun in her (Philippians 1:6 *KJV).* Complete and finalize her healing. Make this season a thing she barely remembers. *Shatter the stronghold of intractable pain and suffering* (Nahum 1:7 *KJV).* Please thank the holy angels for removing, as per our request, the host of enemy agents assigned to cripple and disable her. Now, Lord, *we ask You to release angelic guards to block the return of even a single one of them. Awaken the angels standing guard for Carol* (Psalm 91:11 *KJV).* Put them on high alert and send other angels to deliver her household, property and automobiles from demonic infestation. Sweep it clean.

Guard and protect her family and keep them under the shadow of the Almighty (Psalm 91:1 *KJV,*) and the Blood of Yeshua! Make them invisible to the enemy. We know the mission prepared for them is dangerous and secret but You have made them great warriors. *Prepare them all in Your hiding place* (Psalm 119:114 *KJV*). Only You can set these plans in motion, only You can bring victory in this clash of kingdoms. We release forgiveness and restoration, shalom, understanding, brotherly love, kindness, and joy upon Your daughter. Amen.

Prayer Ten

Our Father and Lord, We again bring Carol to Your Throne Room. We ask that You accept our sacrifices of prayer and praise. May they rise before You like sweet incense now and forever (Hebrews 13:15 KJV).

The seventh day is sacred and perfect to You; it is the day You ordained for us to rest from our labor and take refuge in You (Exodus 20:8-11 *KJV*). May Your rest encompass Carol. Take her to Your secret chamber and heal her. Restore health, restore her tired body and her damaged and traumatized brain; restore every synapse, every ganglion, every cell. Restore her vision, restore her vestibular system and her balance. Restore youth, restore beauty, restore joy, and be her strength. Thank You for loving her and for extending Your mercy and kindness to Your precious child. Remember her mission and equip her with everything she needs to bring Your plans for her to completion (Hebrews 13:21 *KJV*).

We celebrate You today, *King of Kings, Lord of Lords, our Creator, Counselor, Redeemer, Healer and Friend* (Revelation 19:16 *KJV*). *All dominion, power and grace belong to You* (Psalm 22:28 KJV). Amen.

Chapter Five

Prayers Eleven to Twenty-One

"Yet the Lord longs to be gracious to you: therefore he will rise up to show you compassion. For the Lord is a God of justice. Blessed are all who wait for him" (Isaiah 30:18-NIV!)

Injunction for Relief

We petition the Court of Heaven and enter an Injunction of Relief against the prince of darkness, "the powers, and principalities, evil rulers of this age and wicked spirits in heavenly places" (Ephesians 6:12 *KJV,*) who are causing life threatening illness and injury to Carol. These entities are acting in violation of the laws of the Court of Heaven. Such laws state that *Carol, through her confession of faith in Jesus Christ (Yeshua the Messiah), has been adopted and sealed as a son of God and a member of His household* (Ephesians 1:13 *KJV*). *She has full rights of inheritance for all the promises made in the will and testament of God* (Ephesians 1:11 *KJV*).

She has been given power and authority over all the power of the enemy and is promised nothing can by any means harm her (Luke 10:19 *KJV*). In violation of this right, these entities are in fact hurting her and trying to end her life by causing, among other things, intractable pain, visual and auditory disturbance, despair and depression.

We entreat the Court of Heaven to intervene immediately and cause the enemy to cease and desist. We praise and thank you in the Name of Jesus, Amen.

Prayer Eleven

Abba, in Yeshua's, Mighty Name we enter Your Presence, You are our hiding place, (Psalm 37:2 KJV,) our fortress and high tower. You are our solid rock, (2 Samuel 22:1-4 KJV,) our anchor in tempestuous times. You surround and enclose us under the shadow of Your wings (Psalm 91: 2-4 KJV). We find our hope, our strength and our very being in You. "We can do nothing without You, but with You, ALL things are possible" (Matthew 19:26 KJV).

We are marking the days, and asking You to put them in Your Book. We want to count them out until Carol is completely healed. Today we release a new beginning for her. We forbid all symptoms of illness and disease. We release her from the need of medication to control pain. We declare that her brain and nerves function perfectly. *You knit her together in her mother's womb. She is fearfully and wonderfully made* (Psalm 139:14 KJV). *You blessed her, You created her to be Your child, a citizen of Your Kingdom* (Ephesians 1:4 KJV). She is healed through Jesus, by whom she is intimately known. *She is healed by His stripes, His sufferings and His broken body* (Isaiah 53:5 KJV). Fulfill these promises as we release blessings in this very hour!

Carol is sealed by the Holy Spirit (Ephesians 1:13 KJV) *and has inherited authority and power over all the power of the enemy, as have we* (Luke 10:19 KJV). We stand in the gap for her, and we ban and condemn the enemy in every manifestation. He is forbidden from affecting her health, family, finances, voice, thinking, resolve, or relationships. Nothing can block her from the blessings You have for her. *We release those blessings and agree with Your Word which says the power of the curse met its death at the cross* (Galatians 3:13 *KJV*). The power of every curse, incantation, chant and murmuring we command to fall to the ground now, dead, void of all powers contained in them. No evil thing can touch her any longer.

We thank You for sending Your angelic hosts *to defend against the powers and principalities arrayed against her* (Ephesians 6:13 *KJV,*) and we destroy the court documents in which the enemy has spoken slander and attempted to impeach her. (Daniel 7: 9-10 *KJV*). Carol is Your ransomed child. "Arise O Lord, Let her enemies be scattered" (Numbers 10:35 *KJV*). See our injunction for relief and act swiftly to restore her to health and vitality. Thank You for Your bountiful love and Your unfailing mercy. *Ride through the heavens to Carol's help* (Deuteronomy 33:26 *KJV,*) and pour into her Your wisdom, grace, kindness and power. Amen.

Prayer Twelve

Abba, we are standing before Your Throne on behalf of Carol. Father, one tiny movement of Your finger can completely heal her.

We release divine healing over her now. We call forth a reversal of the damage to her body and *restoration of her well-being.* (Joel 2:25-32 *KJV).* We speak healing to every nerve, muscle and sinew, every ganglion and synapse. We speak to the mountain of medical evidence and speculation piled up before us; all surgeries, diagnoses and procedures with their deleterious statements and bad reports. We forbid them to adversely affect her activity or her life. We reject all bad reports, failed procedures, and names or titles of diseases. Such things can no longer adversely affect Carol's outcome. We believe Your Word is truth. *She is standing in Your strength* (Nehemiah 8:10 *KJV,) and healed by and through Jesus, her salvation and her song* (Psalm 118:14 *KJV).*

You are her Healer and Deliverer. *There is none like You Who makes the blind see, the deaf hear, and the dead arise* (Matthew 11:5 *KJV).* We have confidence and faith for her complete healing. We trust and expect You will repair or remove all foreign objects, scars, broken pieces, and parts, fears and disappointments. We trust and adore You, for *You are not a man that You would lie* (Numbers 23:19 *KJV).*

We stand in agreement with Your Word and Your character while we wait for Carol's healing. Amen.

Prayer Thirteen

Father, in the Name of Jesus we pray. We come with praise and thanksgiving because You are the source of all our hope, (Psalm 100:4 KJV). You lovingly collect our tears in Your bottles, (Psalm 56:8 KJV). You have heard our cries and decreased our suffering. Thank You for being a faithful and loving Father.

How gracious and kind You are to Your children. What mercy You extend when you reach out Your hand to cure and heal. *Now Father we come again in the powerful, transformational Name of Jesus, who Himself performed signs and wonders for the sick and broken when He was on earth* (Acts 2:22 *KJV*). *He is seated at Your right hand to intercede for those needing healing and help now* (Romans 8:34 *KJV*).

On this day we know Carol has Your attention and we know You will grant her favor, *hear our prayers and heal her from every sign and symptom not in alignment with Your Word* (1 John 5:15 *KJV*). *You tell us worshipping, You, obedience, and walking in Your pathway are health and life to us. They are strength and life to our bodies* (Deuteronomy 5:33 *KJV*). We release an extra measure of the 'heart of worship' to Carol. She follows after You with her whole heart and all her strength. Hear us O Lord and heal her.

Because we have power over the enemy, we stand in our authority and issue a "cease and desist" order from the Courts of Heaven. We serve it at once on Carol's tormentors. We forbid this torment to continue. "If we resist the devil he will flee" (James 4:7 *KJV*). We declare Yeshua, Jesus, "is greater the he who is in the world" (1 John 4:4 *KJV,*) and it is His power that heals and restores. We tear down and destroy every enemy stronghold constructed against her health and well-being and loose the healing power which comes from Jesus our Messiah. We are expecting great things as we pray, stand together and believe! Amen.

Prayer Fourteen

Most Holy God, we "enter Your gates with Thanksgiving and your courts with praise" (Psalm 100:4 KJV). Lord, in the name above all names, the Name of Jesus, we come to You. You are our All in All; You fill all things everywhere with Your presence (Ephesians 1:23 KJV). You are the ALEPH and the TAV, the Alpha and Omega.

You bring us safely through fire and flood (Isaiah 43:2 *KJV*). You shelter us in the storm and shade us in the heat. "You give us hind's feet for high places and cause us to make spiritual progress in our times of trouble, suffering and responsibility" (Psalm 18:33 *AMP*). How great You are!

Thank You for being with Carol and for heeding our cries for her help. She stands in need of You right now. She needs insight, revelation, wisdom, and a sound mind, unfettered by pain and unclouded by the medication now required to treat that pain. She needs clarity which can come only from You. She has important decisions to make. She needs to "stand still and see the deliverance of the Lord" (Exodus 14:13-14 *AMP*). You are her best and only option. The best of doctors have not helped her, but You are the Great Physician and You will heal her we know. *You planned in love for her long ago. You chose her before the foundation of the world* (Ephesians 1:4 *KJV,*) and *You have a hope and a plan for her future. It is a plan for good, not for harm* (Jeremiah 29:11 *KJV*). Your plan does not include a life of crippling pain. We call forth Your plan over her life. We call it forth. *We agree with You Lord and we know You will perfect the good work You have begun in her* (Philippians 1:6 *KJV*).

Thank You Father for always inclining Your ear and hearing us when we pray. Amen.

Prayer Fifteen

Dearest Abba, "Our Father, Who art in heaven, Hallowed be Your name. Let Your Kingdom come and Your will be done on earth as it is in heaven" (Luke 11:2-4 KJV).

We know Your will is, and has always been, health for Your people (Exodus 15:26 *KJV).* When You brought Your children out of Egypt not a single one was sick or lame. When You saved and delivered them, You healed them. This is Your will for all Your children. On this we stand.

We come to Your courtroom asking for justice for Carol. She was brought out of her Egypt by the blood of Jesus. She is a sojourner here. *Your Kingdom is her home because she is Your daughter and a citizen of heaven* (Philippians 3:20 *KJV).* We are right to stand in Your court and ask boldly for her healing. This sickness is a plot, strategy and tactic from her adversary, the devil. He must unhand her immediately. She is redeemed, delivered, righteous and healed. No charge or accusation can be brought against her, as all her sins, shortcomings and failings were washed away by the blood of Yeshua. This harassment is illegal. The blood has never lost its power and *You are the same yesterday, today and forever* (Hebrews 13:8 *KJV).*

We rebuke the devil and his demonic host for continuing this illegal assignment and we bring his actions before You and Your Court and ask You, too, to rebuke him. We put You in remembrance of the injunction filed against him and we petition You to cancel the assignments executed against Your daughter.

We proclaim she will have instant relief, deliverance, restitution, and reparation for all suffering inflicted by his hand.

Help us, Father to do, pray, and speak rightly so Carol can find relief. *Thank You Holy Spirit for interceding for us as we pray* (Romans 8:26 *KJV).* Thank You for Jesus and His gracious love and healing power. Thank You for the Holy Spirit who accomplishes all. Amen.

Prayer Sixteen

Praise the Lord! Praise the Lord from the heavens, praise Him in the heights! Praise Him, all His angels! Praise Him, all His hosts! Praise Him, sun and moon! Praise Him, all you stars of light! Praise Him, you highest heavens and you waters above the heavens! Let them praise the name of the Lord for He commanded and they were created. He also established them forever and ever. He made a decree which will not pass away (Psalm 148:1-6 NIV).

Lord, we are standing in prayer for Carol and remind you of all our prayer for her. May they rise before Your Throne and reach Your very heart of compassion. We are grateful You are full of loving-kindness and abounding in mercy. It is Your mercy we need now along with compassion and kindness too. As we stand to proclaim Your Name and Your restoring power we ask You to reach out Your hand to cure and to heal Your daughter. Jesus accomplished her healing two thousand years ago. We pray in His name for her manifest healing.

Lord, when we consider all created beings are commanded to praise You (Psalm 150:6 *KJV,*) we have a hint of Your majesty and dominion. We are not asking anything too hard for You. *You are the God of heaven and earth. You are constant. Your Word is forever established in the heavens. It will not pass away* (Isaiah 30:28 *KJV*). Send forth Your Word to heal Carol.

Thank you Creator, Sovereign and King. Amen.

Prayer Seventeen

Abba, Father, Creator, the Three in One, All in All, High Tower, Strong Defender, Place of Safety, Kingdom Builder.

We come through the door on the narrow way, the door of Jesus, Yeshua, to ask for Your help to reach Carol. *You are The One Who knit her together in her mother's womb! You designed her and You know her every strength and weakness. You created her destiny* (Psalm 139:1,4,13-15 *KJV*). *You placed Your DNA in her and through the blood of Jesus redeemed her from the curse* (Colossians 2:14 *KJV*). She is part of the Body of Christ, the same body to which we, who pray for her, belong. She is hurting and we truly hurt with her. We can't be okay until she is thoroughly and completely healed and restored. You made us all intrinsically connected.

You promised to hear us when we pray. We ask you to incline Your ear as we proclaim and declare the healing power of Jesus over her. Yeshua came to heal and deliver her. Raise her up Lord! One glance, one word, one drop of compassion will be the answer. "Yes" is the answer; "Amen" is the answer (2 Corinthians 1:20 *KJV*). *We know You never waiver or change* (James 1:17 *KJV*). We believe, in every respect, you are breathing health, prosperity, and favor into every aspect of Carol's being.

She has been planting with tears and longs to reap the fruits of the Spirit. Joy, strength, healing and health are bestowed on her as we stand in agreement with Your Word. *We do not fight against flesh and blood, we do not fight each other* (Ephesians

6:13-17 *KJV*). We fight the enemy in all his iterations and we command he step away from her. We forbid his every action directed against her and we release her to wholeness and cure in the Name of Jesus. Jesus is the Name above every name that's been given. His is the Name that shatters strongholds and sets the captive free. We believe, trust and know Carol is made well and we thank You Lord. Amen.

Prayer Eighteen

Abba, Father, You provided us a day of rejoicing! Thank You for good news.

Carol is noticing improvement. We know beyond doubt this is You; You are moving heaven and earth on her behalf. Thank You.

We continue to storm heaven for her because she is still too weak to do it herself. It is our privilege. We come to You praying in the Name of Jesus. *We know You will hear and answer us. She is healed is in accordance with Your will* (1 John 5:14 *KJV*). We know if we pray, "believing that we have, as a present possession, what we ask for, we will have it" (Mark 11:24-25 *KJV*). Today we come believing she is already healed. It is our present possession.

Yes, she still has bad doctor reports, she still has real metal screws in her head, she still has signs and symptoms. We see that in the natural, but today we place our BELIEF in You and Your Word. We believe the supernatural over the natural; we believe the unseen over the seen, and we declare Carol's healing in spite of natural, physical evidence and bad reports. This is because with You all things are possible! This is because *You proclaim over and over that Your Word will never fail and never pass away* (Matthew 24:35 *KJV*).

We obliterate the evil plans, strategies and tactics raised against this family and we ask You to send angels to disturb and destroy the intention of the enemy. *Loose Your divine protection and hide Carol under the shadow of Your Wing* (Psalm 91:1 *KJV*).

Your plans are far greater than any plan the devil can make. Thank You for completely delivering your daughter from the "snare of the fowler" Psalm 91:3 *KJV).* Amen.

Prayer Nineteen

Abba Father, we come again to the courts of Heaven and to Your Throne bringing Your daughter's need for healing. Thank You for being a God who does intervene in the affairs of man.

It's so amazing considering You are omnipotent, omnipresent and all knowing. *We are amazed that You would ever think of us, much less number the hairs on our head* (Luke 12:7 *KJV*). But You do, and *You consider us; though we are dust* (Psalm 103:14 *KJV*).

We know Your thoughts are toward Carol. *You sent Jesus, Yeshua, to claim her and give her a full and abundant life* (John 10:10 *KJV*).

> You are looking and longing and waiting to be gracious to her. You are able to carry out Your purpose and do super-abundantly more than all we dare ask or think, infinitely beyond our greatest prayers, hopes or dreams; according to Your power at work in her (Ephesians 3:20 *AMP*).

That's why we pray believing and why we stand believing. We know our faith will prevail, Your Word will prevail, Yeshua's promises will prevail and Carol's history of pain, persecution and torture will be erased as she walks in the fullness of Your healing, mercy and kindness.

We put You in remembrance of Your Word; *Your calling and*

gifts are irrevocable (Romans 11:29 *KJV).* Carol will prevail and complete the mission You assigned her. The enemy can no longer forestall and detain her. We break every chain, rope and binding grip the devil and his minions have used to try to render her ineffective. In Yeshua's mighty, beautiful and powerful name we declare her healed and set free. Amen.

Prayer Twenty

Abba, how blessed we are to have You as our Father. We come to you in the Name of Jesus, Yeshua, and in agreement with You, believing might and power are not enough; as it is by the Spirit Your plans are brought to completion (Zechariah 4:6 KJV).

Every good and perfect gift comes from You in Whom there is no variation or shadow of turning (James 1:17 *KJV*). *When You start a good work in us, You bring it to perfection and complete it* (Philippians 1:6 *KJV*). You are worthy of all thanksgiving, praise and worship, for You alone are God.

We continue our case for Carol today and call forth a "Healing and Deliverance" Judgment on her behalf. We believe You are honoring our requests for her complete healing and deliverance. You know them all, but I want to remind You: we do not ask for Carol alone, our requests are for Carol the wife, mother, mother in law, sister, daughter, and friend. She fills many critical roles and she is needed and desired by her family. She has a husband who needs his partner, a son and daughters who need her nurturing and guidance, a brother who is counting on her because their missions are interlinked, and parents who need her as they grow old. We thank You for this family, but You can see how one member taken away from them causes all the members to suffer greatly. Our requests for her healing are to the good of all her family. Her restoration will be healthful and beneficial to them all. Her minor children need her most and she often can do nothing for them because of disabling pain. Instruct Your Court to consider all these things when they deliberate the punishment we request be wrecked upon the enemy.

Father, You have sent her into many places of darkness and she has carried Your light, bringing truth into that darkness. For this, she and her family have suffered at the hand of the devil. We beseech You to hear our cries as we contend for her and her family. Restore frayed relationships, restore tired hands and bodies, restore joy; restore her ability to do Your Kingdom's work. *Keep Your angels around her to guard and guide her* (Proverbs 3:6 *KJV*) as You heal and cure her. We know You will heal and restore the whole family. You finish the work You begin and we thank You. Blessed and Holy are You O Lord. We exalt Your name forever. Amen.

Prayer Twenty-One

Beautiful Savior, Prince of Peace, Wonderful Counselor, (Isaiah 9:6-7 KJV,) we come to our Father in Your name, thanking You that we were not left as orphans, but have the Holy Spirit to guide, comfort, and act on our behalf (John 14:26 KJV).

Once again we see that You thought of everything we need. It's an amazing privilege to be part of Your family.

We put You in remembrance of Your Word. You say, "Ask and keep on asking, seek and keep on seeking, if you knock and keep on knocking then You will open the door and give us what we ask and seek" (Matthew 7:7 *AMP)* We are seeking complete healing and total deliverance for Carol. Now we ask, and ask and ask again. We are seeking an answer for her. The doctors don't agree; her family doesn't know what to do; she is worn out but continues on to the point of physical and emotional exhaustion. She has lost her will to fight and her will to live. Hear us this day and heal her we pray. Don't delay another second; speak a resounding YES to her. *Let us all hear You say "YES!" as the devil turns and runs at the sound* (James 4:7 *KJV). (Emphasis added).*

We declare Carol is blessed and satan has no power in her life or the lives of her loved ones. *She is covered by the wings of the Almighty. No evil can come near her dwelling places. Her angels guard her* (Psalm 91:11-13 KJV)) and *You Yourself bless her when she goes in and when she goes out* (Deuteronomy 28:6 *KJV).* You prosper all the work of her hands and all she does comes under Your blessing. *We declare she is strong in the power of Your strength and able in Your capability* (Ephesians 6:10 *KJV*). She has her being in You and she lives a pain free, healthy and joyful life, surrounded by those who love her, care for her, pray for her or depend on her. *She can do all things through You because You strengthen her* (Philippians 4:13 *KJV*).

Thank You for giving her the desire of her heart and for healing her now. "To You be the power, the Glory and the honor forever and ever, Amen" (Revelation 5:13 *KJV*).

Chapter Six

Prayers Twenty-Two to Thirty-Two

Ask and keep on asking and it will be given to you, seek and keep on seeking and you will find; knock and keep on knocking and the door will be opened to you.~(Matthew 7:7 AMP).

Prayer Twenty-Two

We enter Your Courts with praise, Eternal One, in the Name of Jesus. You promised us this Name, above all Names, gives us unfettered access to You (Philippians 2:9 KJV).

We can hardly comprehend a Name above all names. *It's the Name to whom every thing in heaven and earth must bow* (Romans 4:11 *KJV*).

It's the Name with final authority. Jesus told His followers, "ask the Father in My Name and He will answer you" (John 14:13 *AMP).* You are already expecting and waiting to answer us.

Thank You so much for causing Carol to feel hopeful and for improving her mental and physical well being. You are good to do this. Thank You for hearing us and helping her.

Lord, please remember Your word; *the Son of God, Jesus, was made manifest to undo, demolish and destroy the things the devil has done. That is the very reason He came to this world (1 John 3:8 KJV).* It makes us so mad. The devil set up a stronghold against her when she was young, he assigned devils and demons to destroy her and he's been sneaking around hurting her this whole time. Now, we, her prayer team, have found him out and used our Yeshua-given authority to shatter his plans. Look with compassion on the havoc the devil set upon her. Cure her we pray. Now she needs Your Mighty Hand, Your mercy and loving-kindness to settle on her every cell and restore her. Her mission is awaiting her. Restore her today we beseech You.

We decree she has been set free from every snare and trap. Her brain, cells, nerves, white matter, ganglia, and every structure of the nervous system are now infused with the stem cells of The Most High. Her healing and deliverance is set upon her and anything foreign in her body is removed in the Name of Jesus. She is walking on the path to perfect health. Thank You Lord. Amen.

Prayer Twenty-Three

Our Father in heaven, "Your name is hallowed; may Your Kingdom come and will be done on earth as it is in heaven. Give us this day our daily bread" (Matthew 6:9-12 AMP) We gratefully receive our Daily Bread, Your Word.

We thank You for Your Word; *Your Word which never passes away; Your Word Who dwelt among us; Your Word made flesh so we could understand it* (John 1:14 *KJV*). We "do not live by bread alone but by EVERY word proceeding from Your mouth" (Matthew 4:4 *KJV*). *(Emphasis Added).* Your Word is our very life. Your Word, Jesus, has conquered even death. *You sent forth Your Word and He healed us* (Psalm 107:20 *KJV*). Thank you for moving heaven and earth so we could be made whole. This is Your will.

In this context we understand that, though we are the ones interceding for Carol, it's Your Word which avails for her. Jesus is the source of healing and shalom. He is the Prince of Peace. In Him nothing is missing, nothing is broken and nothing is lost.

We declare His perfect peace to Carol. We declare nothing of discord or chaos is allowed in her body. We declare: every misbehaving and foreign cell, nerve or process is banished from her body. Her body and brain put themselves into alignment for perfect healing and peace. No interloper or usurper is allowed permission to remain. Your perfect peace, grace, healing, shalom is Carol's today. Thank You for hearing us when we pray. *We stand on the Foundation Stone, believing* (1 Corinthians 3:11 *KJV*). Amen.

Prayer Twenty-Four

Abba! What an honor to call you our Father,
Creator of the Universe.

We come as Carol's intercessors to ask for help in time of need. *You are our ever-present, well timed help* (Psalm 46:1 *KJV*). You are never late and we trust You. We know You always hear when we pray in the mighty Name of Jesus.

Once again we place Your daughter on the alter before You. We need You desperately. You alone can resolve her health issues. Physicians have already opened her skull and moved her brain. She has screws in her head. Her nerves were damaged in the process. Her pain has continued over hours, days, months and years. No human skill has delivered permanent relief for her. *But, You O God, do with ease those things impossible for man* (Matthew 19:25 *KJV*). *You look and long, and wait to do good for Carol* (Isaiah 30:18 *KJV*). Yeshua intercedes for her right now. He took suffering and brokenness in His body so that no power of hell can prevail against her healing and deliverance. What a Savior! *She is the joy set before Him on the cross* (Hebrews 12:2 *KJV*).

We declare her healed and delivered, *not by our power, not by our might, but by Your power and might, and for Your glory* (Zachariah 4:6 *KJV*). How great and gracious You are. We declare her complete and instantaneous deliverance. Demonstrate Your love in this tangible way so all will know beyond doubt You are the Great "I Am."

Let your love, forgiveness and healing wash over Carol and her entire family until they all stand redeemed and fully alive before Your Throne where we stand today. Amen.

Prayer Twenty-Five

"You, O Lord, are a shield for me, my glory and the lifter of my head" (Psalm 3:3 KJV) Abba, while this verse applies to all of us, we ask You to think of Your daughter Carol.

In the mighty Name of Jesus we bring our petition before You.

You are her Shield. You are the One who protects her, who leads her in the way and oversees each step she takes: past, present and future. *You are the One who knows ahead of time, every danger, snare and pitfall along her path* (Proverbs 3:6 *KJV*). You are the One who called her to a dangerous path. You have given her and us "power over all the power of the enemy and NOTHING can by any means harm her" (Luke 10:19 *NIV*). (*Emphasis added*). You are her glory. We have no glory without You. You are "The lifter of her head" (Psalm 3:3 *KJV*). Father, her head is a head only You can lift. Put Your loving, healing hand below her chin and lift her head until her gaze is fixed entirely on You. She has been healed by the work of Yeshua. Confirm that as she looks at You. Her head is filled with pain. Erase it, we pray. Her cranial nerves have been malfunctioning. Restore them to creation perfection, we pray. Her head has been heavy and her eyes downcast. Lift her head, O Lord, to her place of healing and victory. *Give her beauty for ashes. Place a diadem of beauty upon her head and bind up and heal her broken heart* (Isaiah 61:3 *KJV*). Rip off the grave clothes the enemy has been trying to wrap around her and set her at liberty. Grant her a two-fold recompense for her suffering. *Do all this in accordance with Your Word; the Word You forever established in the heavens* (Isaiah 61:7-8 *KJV*). This is the Word we rely on and upon which we stand.

We are grateful for all Your blessings and gifts to us and praise Your name forever. Amen.

Prayer Twenty-Six

Good Morning Abba! What a wonderful amazing thing to call the Creator of the Universe our own Father. You are all wisdom, all knowledge and all understanding (Isaiah 11:1-5 KJV).

Each day allow us to grow more and more into the image of our Savior. We pray in the name of our Redeemer and King Yeshua, Jesus, the Living Messiah and Name above all Names. Hear us when we pray.

We come in need of Your wisdom and understanding as we appear before Your Throne on behalf of Your daughter. Teach us to pray in ways that please You. "Forgive our sins as we forgive others, and keep us from evil. May Your Kingdom come on earth as it is in Heaven" (Matthew 6: 9-13 *KJV*). Bring healing to Carol because Your beloved, *Jesus, already paid the price for her healing* (Mark 1:11 *KJV*). Set her free from pain and suffering and raise her up to carry out the mission You have given her. Rebuke satan and all his minions and remove them from the territory You have given her. We absolutely rebuke and exile him.

Bring her life, and a life worth living, abundant health, prosperity in all her works and bring her joy (1 Kings 2:3 *KJV*). Your mercies are new and Your grace is sufficient for her today. *Set her in a large place* (Psalm 18:19 *KJV,*) and surround her with true shalom.

Thank You for hearing and answering the prayer of our hearts. Amen.

Prayer Twenty-Seven

Abba Father, You say "when the enemy comes in like a flood You will raise a standard against him. You will drive him out and defeat him" (Isaiah 59:19 KJV)

We are asking You to raise that standard right now in Carol's situation. Drive the enemy away and "bring her to Your banqueting house, where the banner over her is love" (Song of Solomon 2:4 *KJV*). Do not allow the enemy to find her.

We are desperate, Lord. We are pounding on the door, we are crying out for Your help. We have prayed, asked, decreed, declared, commanded, and believed. We have filed a petition, asked for Your court's ruling in Carol's favor, reminded You of Your promises and put our faith on the line. Her suffering is unbearable. We see that, so we know You do too. For the sake of Your great Name, and because of the sacrifice of Jesus, heal her now. She cannot be hopeful when she continues to endure this hardship. We need her, her family needs her, her friends need her and Your Kingdom needs her. We implore You to release her healing, relieve her pain, heal her nerves, and remove the shackles this stronghold has placed upon her. (Acts 16:26 *KJV*)

We know you are merciful and just. You intervene in the lives of Your children, You are all-powerful. *You are predisposed to mercy and compassion* (Psalm 119:37 *KJV*). See her suffering and set her free. "Our power is mighty before You for the pulling down of this stronghold" of suffering (2 Corinthians 10:4 *KJV*). We command this stronghold to crumble in the Name of Jesus. It is not acceptable. As You have done for others, do for Carol. *You are no respecter of persons* (Romans 2:11 *KJV*). "With man this is not possible but with You, all things, are possible" (Matthew 19:26 *KJV*). Please bring her out Abba. Carry her to safety, healing and restoration.

Thank you for hearing and answering our prayers and supplications for her just as You promised You would. Amen.

Prayer Twenty-Eight

Abba, Jesus Himself told the disciples "for the Son of Man did not come to destroy men's lives, but to save them" (Luke 9:56 AMP).

What a promise! We pray in the Name of Jesus, as we have been instructed. We know He intercedes for us. *We know He has been with You since the beginning, and we know He came from You expressly to save Carol to the uttermost* (Hebrews 7:25 *KJV*). Thank You for this amazing plan. Thank You for thinking of her at the foundation of the world. *Thank You for the plans You have for her future, plans for her good not for her harm (Jeremiah 29:11 KJV).*

We are standing, believing the good news of Your Word, the good news of a salvation which makes the sinner whole. We are in possession of the good news of a Redeemer who heals, delivers and restores; and of an Abba who loves us. *We know you are one hundred percent reliable and You are entirely dependable* (1 Thessalonians 5:24 *KJV*). You will see us through as You say You will. We have committed Carol to You, and asked You for her healing, so we know without wavering that You will honor Your Word.

Comfort and strengthen her today. Put all disappointment and pain in her past. Restore to her a sound mind; for "she was not given a spirit of fear, but rather a spirit of power and love" (2 Timothy *1:7 KJV).* You are on her side. Send forth Yeshua, Your Living Word, and heal her completely. Now is the day, now is the hour. We choose and decree health and life for Carol. Bless her abundantly and give her peace.

Thank You for Your grace and mercy, thank You for Your enduring love, thank You for hearing and answering our cries for our sister. Amen.

Prayer Twenty-Nine

Abba Father, thank You for another day of life; a day to rejoice and be glad; a day to rehearse Your awesome deeds. We bless Your Holy Name.

Another week is coming to an end and we are still marking the days as we pray for and present Carol to You. We know her healing is on it's way because we know *You always keep Your Word* (Joshua *21:45 KJV*).

As the enemy takes out his biggest weapons in his last ditch efforts to win this battle we resist him, and decree and declare You made Carol whole. "No weapon he raises against you [her] will prosper" (Isaiah 54:17 *KJV*). Every whispering, accusing demon of hell is exposed as a liar and their words are dead when they leave their lips. We have no part of them and grant them no space or cause to operate. We declare we have all power over the plots and plans devised against her and we cancel them now. *Nothing can by any means harm her* (Luke 10:19 *KJV*). *Your angels will bear her up and out of any dangerous trap the enemy conceives* (Psalm 91:12 *KJV*).

We take our shield of faith and our sword of the Spirit which is the Word of God (Ephesians 6:18-17 *KJV,*) and declare Carol healed, delivered and completely restored. Every hindering spirit is removed and bound on earth as in heaven. Every foreign, sick, damaged, wounded or malfunctioning cell is removed from her body by the work of Jesus. Every enemy knee must bow to the Name above all names. Her brain is restored now. Her vision is normal, her thought processes filled with hope and joy. The fruits of the Spirit flow from her. *Your light illuminates her every step and You direct her path* (Psalm 119:105 KJV).

Thank You for never leaving or forsaking her (Hebrews 13:5 *KJV)* and for bringing her safely through this time she's spent in the valley of the shadow of death. You are so good. Amen.

Prayer Thirty

Abba Father, in the name of Yeshua, Jesus, our Redeemer, we pray. You are so gracious to have given Carol this reprieve. We are proclaiming it permanent and the beginning of her manifest healing.

Bless the Lord, o my soul. Let everything within me praise His holy name. Your hand has laid the foundation of the earth and Your right hand has spread out the heavens. When You call to them they stand forth together to execute Your decrees (Psalm 103:1 *AMP*).

Incredible! Most certainly You who have such servants as heaven and earth can oversee Your daughter's complete healing!

Lord, You say You will help us. By trusting You we will neither be ashamed or confounded (Isaiah 45:17, 54:4 *KJV*). We keep our face set like a flint on Carol's healing, we stand together and *we know You will not shame us for believing* (Romans 10:11 *KJV*). *We do not fear, as we know You are our Rock, our deliverer and our place of safety* (Psalm 18:2 *KJV*). Thank You.

Lord, be Carol's help; let her rejoice under the shadow of Your wings. Let her follow hard after You and may Your right hand uphold her. *Perform on her behalf and bring to pass and complete Your purposes for her life* (Isaiah 46:11 *KJV*). We declare she has heard of Your great promises and puts her faith and trust in You. We declare *You have delivered her from death to life and kept her from falling* (Jude 1:24 *KJV*). *We declare she walks before You in the light of life and of the LIVING* (Psalm 56:13 *KJV*). *(Emphasis added). The* strategies and plans of the enemy are null and void and she is healed.

We rejoice in You our King and praise You. May Your glory fill the earth. Amen.

Prayer Thirty-One

Glorious Father, Strong Defense, Place of Safety, Shield, Lord of the armies of heaven, in Yeshua's name we come to Your Throne Room to worship You and to make our requests known to You.

You told us not to rest until Carol's healing is accomplished. We are realizing how very much you love her and how important her healing is to You. This fills us with faith and hope. So it is with that faith and hope we declare she will have a wonderful, pain free life from this day forward. *Now is the day of salvation and deliverance (2* Corinthians 6:2 *KJV).* The waiting is over and she is fully restored to her family and those who love her. "You have created her anew with eternal seed bought for her by the blood of Jesus" (1 Peter 1:23 *AMP).* The shackles, chains, and imprisonment are now things of the past. *She is free indeed* (John 8:36 *KJV).* She walks in new authority because she knows *You always perform Your Word* (Jeremiah 1:12 *KJV).*

> She understands more clearly the wonders of Your person and is becoming acquainted with the power out flowing from the resurrection of Jesus. She is forgetting what lies behind and is straining forward to grasp what lies ahead (Philippians 3:13 *AMP).*

Father, we do not have anxiety nor do we fret, because we

know You are God in every circumstance and situation. Bring Carol the perfect peace only You can provide. *Thank You for lifting her and carrying her, and all of us, through the tests, tumults, and storms of our lives* (Isaiah 43:2 *KJV*). Thank You indeed.

All Praise, glory, honor and dominion belong to You. Amen.

Chapter Seven

Prayers Thirty-Two to Forty-Two

*For this is what the high and exalted One - He
who lives forever, whose name is holy says: I
live in a high and holy place, but also with
the one who is contrite and lowly in spirit,
to revive the spirit of the lowly and to revive
the heart of the contrite~(Isaiah 57:16 NIV).*

Prayer Thirty-Two

God and King, Lover of My Soul, El Shaddai, Adonai, we bless and exalt Your Holy Name and approach You in the name and through the blood of Yeshua, Jesus.

"This is a day You have made and we rejoice and are glad in it" (Psalm 118:24 *KJV*). This is a day to eat, drink and be merry. *This is a day of thanksgiving to You for Your marvelous deeds and Your loving kindness* (1 Chronicles 16:24 *KJV*).

Be especially near to Carol today. Keep Your hand upon her head and heart. Send the healing power of Jesus to flow over her from head to toe as she walks in victory over pain. We thank You that she is so loved, so adored and so respected in the halls of heaven. You are the Creator and she is Your creation. You breathed into her nostrils the breath of life.

> You created her in Your own image (Genesis 1:27 KJV). "Your eyes saw her unformed substance. You knit her together in her mother's womb. and before a word is on her tongue, You know it. "She is fearfully and wonderfully made" *(Psalm 139:13-16 KJV).* Give her an open heaven and honor all her requests. Help her surrender her burdens to you, give her peace and refreshment as You *fit her with Your yoke which is easy and light* (Matthew 11:33 *KJV*).

Command Your angels to serve, care for, protect, and watch

over Carol. We praise You Father, Lord of Heaven and Earth. We openly and joyfully acknowledge Your great wisdom and we submit ourselves to Your purposes and will for our lives. Blessings, glory and honor forever belong to You. Amen.

Prayer Thirty-Three

In the beginning was the Word. In Him was Life and the Life was the Light of men. The Light shines on in darkness for the darkness has never overpowered it, absorbed or appropriated it (John 1:1 AMP).

Abba Father, Carol is in an epic struggle between Light and Darkness. *Thank You for Your promise which tells us darkness will never win. Your light always overpowers darkness* (John 1:6 *KJV*).

Thank You for healing her on this Shabbat morning. We are grateful for every victory and every pain free moment, but we need Carol to separate completely from the pain being inflicted upon her and be free of it for the remainder of her life. We command, in Your name, pain to leave at once and not return.

Thank You for her deliverance. *Give her a heart of gladness today. Place upon her Your garment of praise and erase heaviness and grief* (Isaiah 61:1 *KJV*).

Thank You, Lord of the Sabbath, for giving her a resting place today. Amen.

Prayer Thirty-Four

Great is Your name O God! You fill all things everywhere with the power of Your Presence. In You all Glory resides Ephesians 1:23 KJV).

We approach Your Throne in the name above all names, the name of Yeshua, Jesus.

Hear our entreaties and pleas for Carol's deliverance. Hear our requests, our knocks, our calls and cries. Add them all up, weigh them, measure them and deliver her today (Psalm 34:17 *KJV).* Provide total deliverance; complete and total healing, nothing, not a single cell, should be omitted. Heal every afflicted cell in her body according to Your powerful Word. Set Your Holy Spirit upon her in a new and powerful way. Saturate her with abundant love and abounding good health. Flood her heart with encouragement and happiness. *Be her strength and her salvation* (Psalm 118:14 *KJV).*

We have called to You O Lord, to break her from her pain prison, just like the angels broke the chains off Paul and Silas. These chains are no less real than those. *Lay her chains on the prison floor and send Your angels to escort her out and restore her to her loved ones* (Acts 16:26 *KJV).*

We thank you for being the same, yesterday, today and forever (Hebrews 13:8 *KJV).* Make Your daughter whole and we will rejoice and give all the credit to You. Amen.

Prayer Thirty-Five

Three in One: Jehovah Rophe, our Healer, Deliverer and Friend; All in All, Eternal God. Almighty One; We come to You in the Name above all names, the Name of Jesus.

We are standing, praying and believing that Carol's healing and deliverance are a priority to You.

We have a sense of urgency telling us, NOW is the time for her to *run and not be weary, to walk and not faint* (Isaiah 40:31 *KJV*). Now is the time for strength to return and abound. We have waited for You Lord and we know that You are renewing her strength and power so she can run the race before her.

In accordance with Your Word; we agree together that she is in perfect health. Let her walk in divine health here on earth. We call forth shalom, perfect wholeness and rest for her. We forbid demonic interference, we forbid outbreaks of pain and disability, we forbid discouragement and disappointment and in their place we loose faith and joy; peace and love over her. We celebrate her gifts and declare a new and more powerful anointing for Your glory. We forbid the symptoms of double vision, vestibular interference, nerve pain and other ailments, along with her sorrow, guilt and regret. *We loose over her every spiritual blessing in the heavenly realm and every supply and blessing she needs on earth* (Ephesians 1:3 *AMP*). This is Your daughter, *the joy set before You on the cross* (Hebrews 12:2 *AMP*). Act on her behalf because You are compassionate and good. Thank You. Amen.

Prayer Thirty-Six

Everlasting Father, Mighty God, in the Name of Jesus, and for His sake, we stand together, contending for Carol's freedom. We won't and can't give up. You are good, You are wise, You are merciful and kind. Hear us and answer us on her behalf.

We ask You to dispatch Your angels to remove every obstacle and hindrance in her path. We bind every evil spirit assigned to torment her. *We have, through prayer and supplication, made our petitions known to You* (Philippians 4:6 *KJV*). We cleared the way, Lord, for You to act. *We believe it is Your heart's desire to heal and restore her completely* (Psalm 105:37:147:3 *KJV*). Please do it now so You don't have to share Your glory with a doctor or anyone else. We want to stand amazed when we see her well and her family rejoicing over what You have done for her.

We have used Your Word like a hammer from the very first day we set out to pray. You told us Your "Word will break into pieces even the rock of most stubborn resistance" (Jeremiah 23:29 *AMP*). This is one stubborn rock but we know tough jobs are Your specialty. Be the God of breakthrough this very day and *reach out to cure, heal and restore Carol* (Isaiah 43:19 *KJV*).

We declare and decree she is standing, blossoming with good health, ready to accomplish her mission. *The gates of hell will not prevail against Your good pleasure* (Matthew 16:18 *KJV*). No evil plot or plan of the enemy can cause her to deviate from her calling. She is strong. You are her teacher and the lover of her soul. She is healed and filled with peace and joy. She trusts You and walks in faith knowing she is safe in Your hands. She listens for the sound of Your voice and acts on Your wise commands.

Thank You Yeshua, our King of Kings. Amen.

Prayer Thirty-Seven

*Abba, Holy Spirit, we welcome and adore
You as we pray in the Name of Names, Jesus,*

Our beloved sister and friend is still waiting and watching for You. She's expecting You to act on her behalf.

Father, Jesus came to set the captives free from the bondage brought by the devil. He is our change maker, our rope breaker, our sin taker. He frees and delivers us so we can boldly come before You, washed in His precious blood and made holy through Him.

Today I agree with Him and declare to You Carol is *not a bond-slave any longer. She is set free from all the works the devil has done* (Galatians 3:28 *AMP*). She is saved to the uttermost; thus delivered from illness, guilt, shame, and self recrimination. *There is NO condemnation for she is in Christ Jesus* (Romans 8:1 *KJV*). *(Emphasis Added)*. The past is past, the day of salvation, deliverance and healing is today. Her future is fully committed to You. You direct her path, You are the life she longs for, You are the answer to all things. *The enemy is as powerless as dust and cannot touch or harm her* (Luke 10:19 *KJV*).

Thank You Father for this tangible demonstration of Your great love towards her. Thank You for deliverance and wholeness, for mercy and kindness. You are the power behind our breath, the song in our heart and our greatest hope. Amen.

Prayer Thirty-Eight

Most Blessed of all; King of Kings, Lord of Lords, Great and Eternal One, by the grace of Jesus, Yeshua, we are still here, entreating You to hear and answer our prayers for Your daughter and servant.

We stand on the foundation of Your Word which tells us all things are possible with You and nothing is impossible (Mark 9:23 *KJV*). You are far above our adversary. He is nothing compared to You. *His strength and power is limited while Yours is limitless* (Philippians 4:13 *KJV*). We have taken our stand for Carol. "We are looking and longing and waiting for You to act" (Isaiah 30:18 *KJV*). We know You will not bring us to shame for proclaiming Your goodness, mercy and matchless love. We know You are filled with loving kindness and because of that You will deliver and heal her completely. *We know You desire only good for her because You planned a future for her that does not harm her* (Jeremiah 29:11 *KJV*).

We thank You for never leaving her, never forsaking her, never turning away from her (Deuteronomy 31:8 *KJV;*) but rather *running to her when she asks for help* (Psalm 145:18 *KJV*). Thank You she walks in health and prosperity and executes great exploits for Your Kingdom. Hell has no say and holds no sway over her. She is free of crippling pain and requires no medication. She does what You created her to do and serves her family and friends with talent, ingenuity and love. She is whole.

Thank You for hearing us on her behalf. Praise, honor and glory belong to You. Amen.

Prayer Thirty-Nine

Abba Father, many days now have been spent at the foot of Your Throne for the sake of Your daughter!

Father, *when Daniel asked for Your help it was only delayed twenty-one days* (Daniel 10:13 *KJV*). We are experiencing a far greater delay. You say You are no respecter of persons. We know You are sending Your help to Carol right now. *We are looking, and longing, and expecting, You to raise Your mighty arm in her favor* (Isaiah 33:2 *KJV*).

It is right and good You should help and heal her in accordance with Your Word, through the stripes of Jesus and for the sake of Your Great Name.

Please listen to and heed the prayer and the supplications of Your servants. *For Your own sake cause Your face to shine upon Your daughter* (Psalm 119:135 *KJV*). O Abba, incline Your ear and hear:

> "'O Lord, hear! O Lord, forgive! O Lord give heed and act! Do not delay, for Your own sake*" because Carol is Your daughter and is called by Your name* (Daniel 9:19 *KJV*).

Father, please remember the calling and anointing on Your daughter. We remind You of her mission. We remind You "healing is bread for Your children" (Matthew 15: 22-29 *KJV*). We remind You the devil has been trespassing into this family. *We agree with Your Word as we command him to cease and desist* (James 4:7 *KJV*). *We remind You that we have been seeking first You, Your Kingdom and Your righteousness. You promised all these things would be added according through Your riches in glory.* (Matthew 6:33 *KJV*). We stand fast, trusting the certain victory You promised.

Thank You for Your bountiful mercy which is new each morning (Lamentations 3:23 KJV).

In Yeshua's name we present all these requests and supplications to You. Amen.

Prayer Forty

Abba Father, Thank You for being our Hope, our Comfort and our Strong Tower. We come before Your Throne in the Name of Jesus.

We really didn't think we would be here today; spending yet another day of entreating You on Carol's behalf. We thought her pain and debilitating symptoms would be resolved and behind her. We thought You would have reached out and lifted her up and healed her before now. We admit we are disappointed. We know we only see things from our own point of view, not from Yours. *The only option now is to continue with prayer and supplication, add fasting, and wait* (Mark 9:29 *KJV*). You promised You would only do good for her and we are standing on that. *You promised her a future and a hope* (Jeremiah 29:11 *KJV*). We are standing on that. You promised her healing through the stripes of Yeshua (Isaiah 53:5 *KJV*). We are standing on that. We speak life to her. We speak living, vitality, health and deliverance. We are standing on those words and on Your promises (Proverbs 10:11 *KJV*). We believe in her healing. We believe in Your power and might and in resurrection power. We pull Carol from her present situation and declare her free from the bondage of pain. This is the devil's work and he has no authority over us (Luke 10:19 *KJV*). We trust in, believe in, and rely on You; You, O Lord. We rely on You! No man has been able to do what we ask, only You. Please act now and heal Your daughter.

We are unwavering in our love toward You. We adore You and trust Your Word. Amen.

Prayer Forty-One

Abba Father, what an amazing Father You are! You know us. We don't even know ourselves but you know and see all things and know us perfectly. Thank You for taking notice of us. (Psalm 115:12 AMP).

Hear us O Lord, in the Name of Jesus, and be merciful to us and to Carol. Heal and deliver her. Set her free (John 8:36 *KJV)*. Give her the desires of her heart. Work a miracle in her life right now. We pray, believing Your timing is perfect. "You are our ever-present, well-timed help" (Psalm 46:1 *AMP)*. Lord, *You are close to the broken hearted and the crushed* (Psalm 34: 18 *KJV)*. Be close to her. You say "though we confront many evils, You will deliver us from them all" (Psalm 34:19 *KJV)*. Deliver her. "Contend with those who contend against her. Stand up for her help" (Psalm 35:1 *KJV)*.

> Awaken to her cause. Don't let her enemies gloat over her suffering. Take pleasure in the prosperity of Your servant and show [her] Your favor. Let them be confounded who seek to destroy her. Show Your power and might and drive her enemies backward (Psalm 35: 23-26 *AMP)*.

You are our King, O God. Please command deliverance and victory for Your daughter today. Amen.

Prayer Forty-Two

Abba Father, in the Name of Jesus; the Name of He who is seated at Your right hand, far above all powers and principalities and above every other name, we pray (Ephesians 1:21 AMP). Incline Your ear and hear us O Lord.

We carry Carol to Your feet again today. Father, she had a very difficult and painful week and is so discouraged and downcast. Please have mercy on her today, comfort, deliver and heal her.

Father, according to Your Word you will do far above and beyond anything we could ever ask or think (Ephesians 3:20 *AMP)*. We trust Your Word and believe You will do even more for Your daughter than we ask. Our constraints are no barrier to You. You don't need us, but we need You. We aren't asking for anything we can do on our own. We require and need You as we need air to breathe. We can't live without You and your daughter can't be healed without You. Glory, praise and honor are Yours alone. *We worship You. You alone are worthy* (Psalm 145:3 *KJV)*.

Show Yourself mighty and merciful on her behalf and deliver her to health and to her family (Psalm 147:5 *KJV)*.

Thank You, Abba, for hearing and answering our prayer. Amen.

Chapter Eight

Prayers Forty-Three to Fifty-Three

Yours, O Lord, is the greatness and the power and the glory and the victory and the majesty, for all that is in the heavens and the earth is Yours, Yours is the Kingdom, O Lord, and Yours it is to be exalted as head over all~(2 Chronicles 29:11 AMP).

Prayer Forty-Three

Almighty God, maker of heaven and earth, it is You who ordered the universe with Your mighty Word of Power. It is You who spoke to Noah, closed the mouths of Lions, delivered Shadrach, Meshach, and Abednego from the fiery furnace, and raised Jesus from the grave.

We stand in awe of Your Majesty, marveling that every knee will bow and every tongue confess that Jesus Christ is Lord (Romans 14:11 *KJV*). It's because no one else is worthy of or able to withstand all praise.

We are so grateful You take pause and hear us as we pray. We are so grateful *You taught us to come boldly into Your Throne Room* (Hebrews 4:16 *AMP,*) *and to ask and keep on asking* (Matthew 7:7 *KJV*). We are so grateful You gave us Yeshua, our Redeemer and the one true path to You. Thank You.

We are visiting You on behalf of Your beloved daughter. Hear us O Lord, as we lift our voices to You. Heed our requests for her healing and restoration. Deliver her from the evil gripping her head and face. Reach out Your mighty right hand and free her from the pain which imprisons her. Set her at liberty. Your Word says, "Where the Spirit of the Lord is, there is liberty" (2 Corinthians 3:17 *KJV*). The Spirit of the Lord is within her now. May that Spirit, at once, set her at liberty from pain and it's resulting isolation. Return her, one hundred percent whole and healed, to her loved ones. Make her anew, O Lord, and give her shalom.

We love and trust You. Send Your Word to heal her and *work everything together for her good* (Romans 8:28 *KJV)*. Thank You Abba for answering our prayers with a "yes and amen" (2 Corinthians 1:20 *NLT)*. Amen.

Prayer Forty-Four

Good Morning Abba, we enter Your gates with Thanksgiving and Your courts with praise (Psalm 100:4 KJV). Thank You that the veil was rent in two (Matthew 27:51 KJV) and we are in the Holy of Holies to petition directly on behalf of Your daughter.

Our High Priest is Jesus Himself and He is interceding on our behalf even now (Hebrews 5:6 *KJV*).

Hear us O Lord, as we entreat You to heal, cure and deliver Your daughter. Hear us as we remind You there is none like You, full of mercy and abounding in love. *There is none other than the blood of Jesus by which we are brought near* (Ephesians 2:13 *KJV*). *There is none other than Jesus by whose stripes we are healed* (Ephesians 2:10 *KJV*). There is none other than You who planned from the beginning to do good to her. We are waiting for You, trusting and believing Your Word. *This is the foundation upon which we stand* (1 Corinthians 3:10-15 *KJV*).

Pour out Your mercy for Carol. Just as the blood of the Lamb was on the placed upon the Mercy Seat, let Your outpouring of mercy free her from the chains of sickness and pain.

We believe. No one else can do this. We adore You. Amen.

Prayer Forty-Five

Most beloved Abba, we are so honored to be Yours. You chose us as Your children before the foundation of the world. You planned beforehand for Carol and set Your love upon her (Ephesians 1:4 AMP).

You designed a plan of hope and good for her before she was born (1 Peter 1:3-4 *KJV*).

Now the adversary of our lives has taken position against her and we come in the Name of Jesus to petition for her release (John 10:10 *KJV*).

Strengthen her hands and make firm her knees, say to her 'Be strong and fear not. Behold your God will come with vengeance; with recompense He will come and save you.' Then she will leap and sing with joy; for waters will break forth in her wilderness and streams in her desert. (Psalm 35:3-6 *AMP*).

"You give power to the weak and increase the might of he who has no strength" (Isaiah 40:29 *AMP*).

Carol embraces You for her healing and deliverance and so do we, who ask on her behalf. *Healing is bread for YOUR daughter Carol* (Matthew 15: 22-29 *KJV*). *(Emphasis added).* Grant her the wholeness she seeks. Rebuke the devourer and restore her to the fullness of life. She is unable in her own strength to praise You from a bed of pain. Allow her to see Your desire toward her and Your strength in her.

May this be the day of her freedom.

Thank You, Abba. We bless Your Holy Name forever. Amen.

Prayer Forty-Six

Abba, if ever we needed You, the big and mighty God, it's right now. If ever we needed a God so powerful He could break every law of nature and reach down to Carol and fix every single thing that is out of place or malfunctioning within her, it is now. If ever we needed Your mercy, it is now.

We just feel we can't wait any longer for her to grasp on to her healing. It seems to us urgent, an emergency. *She's suffering so much, Lord, isn't it just breaking Your heart* (Psalm 56:8-9 *KJV?) We know You take pity on Your children. Hear us O Lord, and heed our cries for help* (1 Peter 5:7 *AMP*). It's difficult to wait any longer because our hearts are broken over her pain and despair.

You are glorious, and excellent and righteous in all Your ways. All glory and honor accrue to You. You do things Your way and we are at a loss to explain, *but we know You love us with an everlasting love* (Psalm 103:1 *KJV*). You will never leave us or forsake us. Right now, Your daughter is feeling alone and forsaken. *Draw near to her, comfort her, speak to her, fulfill Your promises in her* (Jeremiah 31:3 *KJV*). Please heal her completely as she is Your beautiful child and she needs You. We ask You in the Name of Jesus. He is interceding for her, the Holy Spirit is interceding for her and so are we. Hear us O merciful Father. Amen.

Prayer Forty-Seven

Dearest Abba, in Yeshua's name we pray. You are the Great I Am. You are the Aleph and the Tav. Everything starts and ends in You. You are Sovereign in all the Universe and what You decree comes to pass (Isaiah 46:10 KJV).

You spoke the worlds into being and made everything that has been made. With Your voice You made it, separating light from darkness, ordering the stars and seas and calling Your creation good. With Your hands and breath You made us. You fashioned us Yourself (John 1:1-5 AMP). *You showed such care when You shaped us from dust and bone* (Genesis 2:7-8 KJV). You breathed Your breath into us and created in us a speaking spirit. *We are in Your image, reflecting You as we bow before You to pray* (Genesis 1:27 KJV). Incline Your ear to us as You inclined Your ear to Adam, Noah, Abraham, Moses, Samuel, David, Solomon, Isaiah and all Your people through the span of time. You are no respecter of persons. *The blood of Jesus has grafted us, too, into Your household.* (Romans 11:17 KJV). Incline Your ear to us today and grant divine healing to Your daughter Carol. We need Your majesty, blessing and favor if we are to survive. Amen.

Prayer Forty-Eight

Lord Shabuoth, El Shaddai, we are entreating you on behalf of Carol. We are requesting your angel armies be released to her defense immediately (Psalm 84:9-12 KJV).

Send them to remove every evil force aligned against her and her family. These evil assignments are canceled, and are null and void. *Carol is from a line of Priests and Kings, a daughter in the Kingdom of Heaven and Your child* (Exodus 19:6: 1 Peter 2:9 *KJV).*

There is illegal activity being brought against her and it is producing chaos. There is an enclave of wicked spirits conspiring against her and we ask Your angel armies to disband it and banish them and every other force of evil trying to destroy her life. We will not abandon our faith in believing for her healing and deliverance.

Send angels to protect her family and other loved ones. Let angels draw around her bed forming a shield and defense around her. *You promised You would not give us more than we could bear* (1 Corinthians 10:13 *KJV).* You promised You "would rescue the righteous and deliver them from every trial and danger" (Psalm 107:6-9 *KJV).*

We are depending on Your Word and *we know You will never embarrass us or bring us to shame* (Romans 10:11 *KJV).* You are pleased to hear and answer our prayers so we ask You to deliver and rescue your daughter from this terrible trial. *Comfort her and release her from the grip of her affliction. Encourage her and put a song in her heart* (Exodus 15:20 *KJV).*

In You, we are promised a surpassing victory and we claim it. Grant her victory over this trial.

Bring her out and bear her up in Your arms. Let this be the day she finds and enters into Your promised rest and is forever freed from the nerve pain which has been terrorizing her. We rebuke these cellular-level terrorists and command them to leave her at once and forever.

Abba, We are looking to You because "without You we can do nothing, but with You all things are possible" (Matthew 19:26 KJV). Thank You so much for hearing our prayer and answering with a resounding YES. Amen.

Prayer Forty-Nine

Abba, we have seen Your greatness throughout the worlds and universes, in nature and in our own lives. We know beyond question You are merciful and mighty. We thank You for considering us and for allowing us to approach You without fear of reprisal. Thank You.

Jesus, it's in Your name we "come boldly to our Father's throne to ask for help in time of need, and to make our petitions known" (Hebrews 4:16 *AMP*). Without You we would have no access. (Ephesians 2:13 *KJV*). It is through Your pure sacrifice we are able to call on our Father for Carol. Thank You for the great work of salvation.

You instruct us "to bind on earth what is bound in heaven and to loose on earth what is loosed in heaven" (Matthew 18:18 *KJV*). Today we loose healing over Carol. We loose deliverance, we loose divine answers of "Yes" to Your promises of abundant life. We loose health and restoration *of all which has been stolen from her during these years of suffering* (John 10:10 *KJV*). *We loose the light of Yeshua to illuminate her pathway* (John 1:4 *KJV*). We loose her from the bonds of pain, from nerve damage, from headaches, from light sensitivity, from barometric sensitivity, from nausea, from head pounding, from fear of what's coming next, from desperation, from hopelessness, and from despair. We loose vitality and wholeness, shalom and recovery to her. We release energy and stamina, joy, and blessing.

We bind every evil spirit sent to assail her, we bind the spirit of infirmity and those who travel with it and enjoin it from taking further action concerning her. We bind nerve spasms and pain. *We bind the lying tongue of the enemy and his words of death and despair* (Proverbs 18:21 *KJV*). We bind every gossiping, whispering tongue with destruction in its mouth whether intentional or accidental. We bind every curse whether spoken with or without knowledge, including those she's spoken over herself. We bind every negative word.

We loose words of life. "Death and life are in the power of the tongue" (Proverbs 18:21 *KJV*) so we release people to speak life over her. We release life and a life worth living over her. *You, O Lord, will not allow Yourself to be mocked* (Galatians 6:7 *KJV*). You WILL have victory and show Yourself mighty and merciful on her behalf.

Thank You for always hearing us, never leaving us, and always working everything together for our good. You are amazing. Amen.

Prayer Fifty

Abba Father, we are in Your Throne room on the authority of Jesus, on behalf of Carol. We worship and praise You for never leaving us. We know You are Sovereign in all things and Your Word will not return void (Isaiah 55:11 KJV).

Thank You for regarding us and hearing the cries of our heart and the sound of our voices. You are wonderful beyond measure. We have another emergency request. Doctors and procedures have failed again! Carol is discouraged. *In Christ alone our hope is found* (1 Corinthians 15:22 *KJV*). You alone can heal her, help her and set her free. We turn and put all our trust and faith in You and Your plan for her future. *We know it's to help her and not to harm her* (Jeremiah 29:11 *KJV*). Strengthen all of us today as we continue to persist in prayer and to trust completely in Your perfect plans.

We are declaring as one voice, one heart and one mind Carol's healing and deliverance. Please free her from pain and complications; make her completely and totally whole in every way. *May perfect peace find its home in her heart* (Isaiah 26:3 *KJV*). Hear us O Lord, in Yeshua's name. Amen.

Prayer Fifty-One

Abba Father, there is no one like You. You are more than sufficient for all our needs. We acknowledge You in all our ways and ask You to direct our paths (Proverbs 16:9 KJV). You alone have a clear picture of what lies ahead so only You can guide us.

We present Your daughter to You, and, anxious for nothing, we roll our cares and anxieties onto You and ask You, in the Name of Jesus, to hear and answer our petitions for her (Philippians 4:6-7 *KJV*).

We petition You to remove her pain. We petition You to re-establish perfect sight in both eyes. We petition You to re-establish perfect nerve function in each and every nerve fiber and most urgently her trigeminal and occipital nerves. *We petition for a renewing of her mind, return of hope, and strengthening of her faith* (Romans 12:2 *KJV*). We petition for a fully functional return to her loved ones. You can do all things; nothing is impossible for You. We believe You and know You are acting on Carol's behalf even now as we agree together for her healing and deliverance. We thank You. *You are not a man that You would lie, but rather Eternal God, who speaks only and always truth* (Numbers 23:19 *KJV*).

Thank You for hearing our petitions and regarding our requests. Amen.

Prayer Fifty-Two

Everlasting Father, Mighty God, Shield and Defender, in the Name of Jesus we come bowing in the brightness of Your Glory (Hebrews 1:3 KJV).

We come with a fullness of joy because *we are Your own children whom You marked before the foundation of the world. You've always been acquainted with us* (Ephesians 1:4-5 *KJV*).

We are desperate right now for You to hear our prayers for Carol. We know You love and treasure her even more than we do. We know *You are her strength in weakness* (1 Corinthians 12:9 *KJV*). We proclaim Your mercy is new every morning and *Your grace is sufficient to see her through* (2 Corinthians 12:9 *KJV*). You know exactly what she needs and we can trust You to bring her back to full and robust health. You will clear her vision, restore her speech and return her to a vessel of perfect design and function. You are a keeper of Your Word and our ever-present help in trouble. Act, O Lord, and do not delay. Please stand up for her, help her and relieve her pain. Amen.

Prayer Fifty-Three

Father God, You are always reminding us You are Sovereign and everything is in Your control, not ours. We can make many plans, but "You are the One who guides our steps and directs our paths" (Psalm 16:9 KJV). Jesus lives within us.

We've been praying for Your daughter, Carol, for many days now. Today we recognize and acknowledge Your Sovereignty in her life. *You designed her, gave her gifts, and Your hand rests upon her. You know absolutely everything about her* (Psalm 139 1-18 *KJV*). You promised to complete the GOOD work You began in her and declared *no one or nothing could ever snatch her out of the Mighty Father's hand* (John 10:28 *KJV*). We believe You. It's You alone who understands what is going on. We cannot. We want her suffering, embarrassment, and sorrow to be done away with immediately and that's what we ask and keep on asking. Let her day of healing and mercy be today. "Bless us indeed O Lord, enlarge our territory. May Your hand be with us to guide us and keep us from evil" (1 Chronicles 4:10 *KJV*). We pray in the mighty Name of Jesus. Amen.

Chapter Nine

Prayers Fifty-Four To Sixty-Four

The Lord your God is in your midst, a Mighty One. A Savior [who saves]! He will rejoice over you with joy; He will rest [in silent satisfaction] and in His love He will be silent and make no mention [of past sins, or even recall them]; He will exult over you with loud singing~(Zephaniah 3:17 AMP).

Prayer Fifty-Four

Abba, it is Resurrection Sunday. This is the day Jesus forever destroyed the power of death. This is the day the grave was rendered powerless and Yeshua, Jesus became the first fruit of those who were raised from the dead (1 Corinthians 15:20 KJV).

It's the reason we come before Your Throne now. *You have delegated to us the same power that raised Jesus from the dead. We have this resurrection power within us and we appropriate it today as we pray for our beloved Carol* (Ephesians 1:19-21 *KJV*). We come before Your Throne to thank You and praise You for the surpassing victory which conquered death and granted us eternal life. We come in the name of He who conquered death for all, Yeshua the Messiah, our healer.

He is the conquering King, the one who nailed the curse of death to His cross that we might live in Him through the eternity of eternities (Colossians 2:14 *KJV*). Thank You for this amazing sacrifice. There is wonder-working power in the blood of Yeshua.

We are firm in our belief that Carol is healed now, today, *because today is the day of salvation [which means being rescued from harm, ruin or loss] (2 Corinthians 6:2 KJV).*

Your very name, Yeshua, means salvation. Save and deliver according to Your Word. You always keep Your promises. Thank you for hearing our prayer. Amen.

Prayer Fifty-Five

Abba Father, we rejoice in You because we know You are perfecting Your plan for Carol's life.

Her help is in You. You alone are her hope (Psalm 124:8 *KJV*). *Help her believe what You say about her; she is loved* (John 3:16 *KJV*). Help her recognize how to stand in her anointing and fulfill her calling. *She is being lied to by the father of lies, the devil* (John 8:44 *KJV*). Cause her to accept and believe what we already know to be true. Confirm her healing and change her thinking.

Be her pain control today. Thank You for each and every improvement in her situation. We know her full healing and deliverance are at hand. "Bless her and keep her and make Your face shine upon her and bring her peace" (Numbers 6:24-26 *KJV*).

"You are our Mighty God and Strong Deliverer. You are our light and our salvation. Whom shall we fear? The Lord is the stronghold of our lives, of whom shall we be afraid" (Psalm 27:1-2 *NIV*)? Amen.

Prayer Fifty-Six

Abba, "how righteous are Your laws and perfect are Your ways" (Psalm 18:30 KJV). We exalt You. You are worthy of all praise, honor and glory. Great things You have done for us.

We are grateful beyond words. Thank You. Thank you for faithfully listening as we pray for Your daughter. *Thank you for readily answering "yes and amen" to the prayers we lift on her behalf* (1 Corinthians 1:20 *KJV*). Today is the day we are expecting a miracle as You heal her from the inside out!

We know the day is coming when Carol will be like a tree planted by water (Psalm 1:3 KJV). She will delight in doing everything You want her to do. She will be ready in every season to bear fruit and to prosper in all her ways. She will thank You with all of her heart and tell everyone the marvelous things You have done (Psalm 96:3 KJV). She will be filled with joy and sing at the top of her voice in praise to You.

You do not ignore those who cry to You for help nor abandon those who search for You (Psalm 27:9 KJV). You are her refuge in this time of trouble. Deliver her so she can sing praises to Your Name at the gates of Jerusalem. You are our hope because we are helpless without You. We implore You to come to her rescue.

"Lord, You alone are our inheritance, our cup of blessing. You guard everything we have. We know You are right beside us, and we will not be shaken" (Psalm 16:5-8 *KJV*). We are praying because we know You will answer. Blessed be the name of the Lord. Amen.

Prayer Fifty-Seven

Abba, we praise You for another day to live and breathe and know You more intimately. Thank You for Your kindness and love toward us. We know it's You who caused us to rejoice and be glad in this day.

Today pour out blessing on Your servant Carol. *Let her feel the length, height and breadth of Your love* (Ephesians 3:18 *AMP*). *Nothing can ever separate her from You.* (Romans 8:38 *KJV*). You are her Guide and Constant Companion. *You are the Light of her life* (John 1:3 *KJV,*) h*er Solace in times of suffering* (Romans 8:28 *KJV,*) her Comforter in times of anxiety, her Stay in times of trouble, her Wisdom in indecision, her Tower in times of fear, her Healer in illness, her Joy in darkness. You are her kinsman Redeemer and her Recompense and Reward. It's amazing.

Be her rest today (Hebrews 4:11 *KJV,*) as she heals and grows stronger. We thank You for completing the work You began in her body and for her healing and victory. *As she waits on You, renew her strength* (Isaiah 40:31 *KJV*). Give her a strong testimony so she is able to overcome the enemy in every circumstance and situation (Revelation 12:11 *KJV*). Be close to her, envelop her in the wings of the Almighty and give her shalom. Amen.

Prayer Fifty-Eight

Abba, You are so good to us, Your earthly children. Thank You for every generous provision and our many blessings. We recognize that all we have comes from You.

We always have more than we need because You are so kind. Hear us as we pray for our sister Carol. We long for her healing and deliverance.

We know "You are looking for Your Word to perform it and we know Your Word never fails to accomplish that for which it was sent" (Jeremiah 1:12:55:11 *KJV*). We proclaim her healed by the stripes of Jesus. We long for her to have an abundant life. You have put *the power of death and life in the tongue* (Proverbs 18:21 *KJV;*) so we speak life and abundant life over her cells, fibers, sinews, muscles, bones and structure. May her "body prosper and be in health even as her soul prospers" (3 John 1:2 *AMP*). We know healing is in Your hand waiting to be poured out. *We ask for recompense of the time and treasure taken from her at the hand of the enemy* (Hebrews 10:35: Isaiah 35:4 *KJV*).

We break the chains that bind her and loose her from her pain, discomfort, worry, guilt and anxiety. We loose praises to You. *We replace the spirit of heaviness with the promised garment of praise* (Isaiah 61:3 *KJV*). No more suffering for our sister, we believe, in Yeshua's name. Amen.

Prayer Fifty-Nine

King of Kings, Lord of Lords, Wonderful Counselor, Mighty God, Prince of Peace, Jesus Messiah, He who lives forever and changes not, we pray in Your name for our sister (Malachi 3:6 KJV).

We agree with each other and You that her shackles are broken and she is free. You have placed Your healing hand upon her and the pain is ALL gone. You have healed her eyes and her vision, rebalanced her face, organized her speech and reversed everything the enemy tried to accomplish to her detriment. We declare her emancipated by the power of God. *You will bandage her, You will revive her, You will raise her up that she may live before You (1 John 5:4 KJV). Let her become personally acquainted with You, let her press on to know and understand fully Your greatness, to honor, heed and deeply cherish You (Hosea 6:3 KJV). Let her be a sweet fragrance which ascends to You, whether among those who are saved or those who are perishing (2 Corinthians 2:15 KJV).* Transform her into the very image of the glory of the Lord so that all who know her will see the zeal of her service.

Bless all who pray for her today and grant us Your Shalom. Amen.

Prayer Sixty

Father, we come in the Name of Jesus with hearts full of thanksgiving and praise. We know all good things come from You (James 1:17 KJV).

Today we ask You to bless Your daughter abundantly. Let this be a day when she feels YOUR presence and knows the power of the Holy Spirit. Her "power is not carnal but, is mighty in You for the pulling down of strongholds" (2 Corinthians 10:4 *AMP). Every power, principality, wicked spirit and evil ruler of this age is under her authority because she is under the authority of Jesus* (Ephesians 6:12 *KJV). Teach us all the faith and stability we need to heal the sick, raise the dead and drive out evil spirits in Your name* (Matthew 10:8 *KJV).* None of us should be suffering at the hands of these liars. We refuse to allow this sustained assault against Carol or her family. Let us quickly recognize the enemy and demolish him before he so much as gets a foot in the door. We will not show mercy to the devil or let him have any success at our expense. We reject and renounce him and refuse to be used to carry out ANY of his plans, strategies or tactics. We know beyond doubt she is healed.

We reject any and all devilish evidence accumulated against her; evidence which has exalted itself against Your Word (2 Corinthians 10:5 *KJV). To the contrary, we stand believing her deliverance is at hand. Nothing and no one can keep her from victory in You* (Deuteronomy 20:4 *KJV).*

We love her and we love You. We want the best for her and we know You do too. We trust You. Amen.

Prayer Sixty-One

Abba, this is the sixty-first prayer you've given us for Your daughter. That's just how important she is to You. Long ago You told Nehemiah to gather his people where the trumpet sounds. There, You said "You will fight" on behalf of Your people. (Nehemiah 4:20 KJV).

We lift our trumpets and proclaim Carol's victory right now. The atmosphere is changed in, around, and over her home. The angels have been summoned to minister to her even as You heal her (Hebrews 1:14 *KJV*). There is a clash of Kingdoms all around us and *she is called to be a light bearer in this hour* (Matthew 5:14-16 *KJV*). Let her hear the summons and respond to the call as health returns to her body. We can't be sick and disabled soldiers, Lord. She requires healing and deliverance today. We need wisdom and health, strength and endurance, cunning and intelligence to do Your work during an enemy occupation. *The night is coming on and Carol is urgently needed* (John 9:4 *KJV*).

Thank You, Father, for those who have been so faithful in this prayer assignment. Bless them today and bring them the desires of their heart. We pray in the mighty and wonderful name of Yeshua, Jesus. Amen.

Prayer Sixty-Two

Abba Father, thank You for every breath we take and for every beat of our hearts. We are indeed "fearfully and wonderfully made" (Psalm 139:14-15 KJV). Your creations are so complete, perfect and intricate.

We can but imagine how complex Carol's brain is, how incredibly delicate her cranial nerve structures are, how interlinked every action and thought is. It's no wonder this is difficult for doctors to resolve. *They didn't make her. But Lord, You did!* (Psalm 139:17-18 *KJV*). You are the perfect surgeon because Your understanding of her brain and nerves is complete. You can fix her instantly, even without looking. Amazing.

We step into the gap (Ezekiel 22:30 *KJV*) for your daughter, and ask You to regard all of our previous prayers on her behalf. Hear, as our sincere cries ascend to You. Please calculate our love and care for her and answer our prayers for her healing.

Allow all of us, to enter Your rest with the great expectation that we will be made whole. Thank You so much our King. In the Name of Jesus we pray, Amen.

Prayer Sixty-Three

Abba, in the mighty Name of Jesus, we agree in prayer for Your beautiful daughter. We thank You for being the faithful God who is both unchangeable and relevant right now, today (Hebrews 13:8 KJV). Please teach us Your ways, soften our hearts and hear us when we pray (Psalm 86:11 KJV).

We know You are The Answer and believe You have released total and completed healing for Carol. *You have shown us how to bring about a total defeat to the enemy of her soul* (John 16:33 *KJV*). We pray for her deliverance and healing to happen today *enabling all around her to see the magnificent work of Your hand* (Psalm 92:5 *KJV*). Thank You for intervening on her behalf and doing what no physician or medical person has been able to do. "Let the earth be filled with Your glory" (Isaiah 6:3 *KJV*). We release her healing from the very halls of heaven and we forbid continuing sickness, malfunction or disease. Thank You, for Jesus never fails. Amen.

Prayer Sixty-Four

Abba Father, we praise and thank You for another day of life (Psalm 118:24 KJV). We know all we have comes from Your hand. You are our source and our Provider (1 Chronicles 29:16 KJV). Without You we can do nothing. You are so very generous, lavish and kind to us (Ephesians 1:7-8 KJV).

We bring Your daughter to You in the matchless Name of Jesus; *"the Name to which every knee will bow and every tongue confess"* (Romans 4:11 *KJV).* He is Lord! Hallelujah! Father, Carol is Your child and our sister. She really needs Your help. You tell us "You are our ever-present and well-timed help" (Psalm 46:1 *KJV).* Please help us now. Alleviate all her symptoms which include numbness, tingling, pain, frozen muscles in her face, eye issues and anguish and depression. We know she feels abandoned sometimes and fearful she won't be healed. We know we would feel all those things were we in the same situation. Please come very near so she feels the touch of angel wings on her face. *Send the Holy Spirit to comfort as You promised You would* (John 14:18 *KJV). Reassure her that she's not been left her or forsaken and You are with her now, aware of her cries of despair and discouragement* (Psalm 118:6 *KJV).* We know You don't want her to suffer. *We believe in her healing as our present possession and we know we have it* (Mark 11:24 *KJV).*

We call forth sound sleep and break the chains of insomnia. We declare rest and restoration are hers.

Thank You for Your love toward us. Renew our minds, heal our bodies and make us whole. Amen.

Chapter Ten

Prayers Sixty-Five To Seventy-Five

In the same way, the Spirit [comes to us and helps us] in our weaknesses. We do not know what prayer to offer or how to offer it as we should, but the Spirit Himself [knows our need and at the right time] intercedes on our behalf with sighs and groanings too deep for words~(Romans 8:26 AMP).

Prayer Sixty-Five

Abba, in the Name of Jesus we come to Your Throne Room. We come to You with gratitude and an understanding of this prayer privilege we were granted as a gift.

Please hear our prayers and send the Holy Spirit to act on Your daughter's behalf. Please relieve her suffering and give her rest and peace. We declare she

> dwells in the secret place of the most High and shall abide under the shadow of the Almighty. We will say of You that You are Carol's refuge and fortress, her God. In You she puts her trust. Surely You will deliver her from the snare of the fowler and from her deadly illness. Give her angels charge over her to keep her in all her ways. Do this because You have set your love upon her, therefore You will deliver her, set her on high because you know her name. We call upon you, answer us, be with her in this trouble. Deliver her and honor her and satisfy her with long life and salvation (Psalm 91:1-3, 11-12; *14-16 AMP*).

Guard her from all the tricks, plans and strategies of the enemy (Proverbs 1:33 *KJV*). *Keep her in the full armor of God so she is able to deflect the fiery darts of the wicked one* (Ephesians 6:16 *KJV*). We declare "old things are passed away and all things are become new" (2 Corinthians 5:17 *KJV*). *Her mind is being renewed as the water of Your Word washes over her* (Romans 12:2 *KJV*). She "Hasn't been given a spirit of fear, but of power, love and a sound mind" (2 Timothy 1:7 *KJV*).

Yeshua came to destroy and undo the works of the devil and we have been given authority over all the devil's plans and schemes. Restore her to wholeness we pray. We give thanks for Your tender mercies and love. Amen.

Prayer Sixty-Six

Abba Father, You are the Father of a Son.

On the last of these days, He spoke to us through a Son, Whom He appointed heir of all, through Whom He also made the spans of space and the universe. He is the radiance of His glory and the exact representation of His nature, and carries everything by the power in His Word" (Hebrews 1:1-3 AMP).

You, our God, are filled with foresight and understanding. You have given us Your Son so we have a relationship and access to You. It is by and through Jesus that You have illustrated the nature of "son-ship" and the meaning of being an heir to all things. *This is a gift He passed along to we who trust Him when He sat down at Your right hand* (Romans 8:14-15 *KJV*).

We pray in the Name of Jesus, and have direct access to Your Throne by doing so (John 14:13 *NIV*). We are well acquainted with the Holy Spirit and realize "it is not by might nor by power but through the Spirit" (Zechariah 4:6 KJV,) by which all things are accomplished. *We thank You for our Comforter and Advisor* (John 14:16-18 *KJV*). Fill us anew with the Holy Spirit we pray. We welcome Him to every conversation, every activity and every prayer. Enhance our understanding to fully grasp the wisdom, grace, kindness, authority and power we have in and through You. Keep us from underestimating You. Don't allow us to falter in our faith and trust because we know You will bring

Your Word to pass. We celebrate our life in You and *thank You for providing everything we have* (Acts 17:28 *KJV*).

We bring Your daughter, Carol, to You. You are her Redeemer. She loves You from the midst of her suffering. She continues to hold out hope for her healing regardless of the evidence presented to her by her own body. *We stand in agreement with her and in hope right alongside her* (Zechariah 9:12 *KJV*). We know "*yes and amen" are Your answer to our entreaties on her behalf* (2 Corinthians 1:20 *KJV*). We know it is Your heart's desire to see her up and praising You for Your mercy and goodness. *We know it is not in Your nature to deny a request in keeping with Your Word* (Ephesians 2:8-9 *KJV*). Send the wind of the Holy Spirit over her now to free and heal her from the chains the enemy of her soul has placed around her. You are our God and we praise and worship You. Amen.

Prayer Sixty-Seven

Almighty, Omnipotent Father, we acknowledge You in ALL our ways, and lean not on our own understanding. You have promised to be a light to us and to direct our paths (Proverbs 3:6-7 KJV).

Our understanding seems so meager and our light so dim by comparison to You. We want You alone to guide and direct us. *We want to be pleasing in Your sight, not the sight of man* (2 Corinthians 8:21 *KJV*).

Help us lay down the things of the world. *You say the wisdom of man is foolishness to You* (1 Corinthians 3:19 *KJV*). It's Your wisdom we need and we ask for it now. *You say not to be confused by men who profess a view different than Yours. It is You who will prevail* (Proverbs 19:21 *KJV*). Help us to see clearly and increase our understanding of the way You do things. Let us be content in waiting and expecting and believing You will act on Carol's behalf. Let us not falter nor faint.

Please hear our prayers for her complete deliverance and healing. Bring her to wholeness and restore to her all that we feared lost, whether physical, emotional or spiritual. You are a God of mercy, compassion and limitless ability. Please take pity on Your daughter in the name of Yeshua and make her once more whole. We love her and we need her to be with us. We need her seeing eyes and hearing ears to be used for You and Your Kingdom.

We know You have heard our petitions and are coming to her rescue right now (Psalm 34:18-19 *KJV*). We appreciate everything You do for us and we know *we were given Your great love as a free gift* (Romans 6: 23 *KJV*). Thank You. Amen.

Prayer Sixty-Eight

Good Morning Abba, we lift our voices and our hands in praise to you this morning. You deserve all the adoration and thanks we can express.

As we praise You, we open our hearts to receive Your anointing and we invite the Holy Spirit to infuse us with truth, comfort and power. Thank You for Jesus and His life giving blood. It is in His Name, above all names, we pray.

We pray You will protect and keep us and keep the enemy with all his lies, tricks and strategies far from us and from Your daughter Carol today. Let this day bring her victory as her healing proceeds and her pain abates. *We know her name is engraved on the palm of Your hand and Your thoughts toward her are more numerous than the sands of the sea* (Isaiah 49:16 *KJV). You guide her with Your mighty right hand* (Isaiah 41:10 *KJV,) and send Your angels to bear her up when the path becomes obscure or difficult.*

Increase her faith, comfort her heart and bring her shalom. You are her All in All. *Surround her with favor as a shield and grant the requests of her heart* (Psalm 5:12 *KJV).* Increase her as the enemy tries to decrease her. Strengthen her as the enemy tries to weaken her. Fill her with Your goodness and power as the enemy tries to harm her and strip her of her gifts. Heal her body as the enemy tries to destroy it. Make known far and wide who You are and what You have done for Your daughter. You alone will be glorified in all these things.

In Jesus Name and with thanksgiving, we pray. Amen.

Prayer Sixty-Nine

We come to You in Yeshua's name, and we invite our Comforter, the Holy Spirit, to join us as we pray. We covet His Presence as we know He accomplishes these things we ask of You.

Cover Your daughter with Your wings and protect her from all the fiery darts the enemy is flinging at her (Ephesians 6:16 *KJV*). She has been given "power over ALL the power of the enemy and nothing can by any means harm her" (Luke 10:19 *NIV*). (*Emphasis added*). We take You at Your Word and declare through You, that she is victorious in battle. We stand with her and reject the enemy. We renounce his actions and loose her from every plot and ploy he endeavors to use. We remember Gideon's small army was triumphant so we know this small army will emerge victorious. You have appointed us and You will see us through.

Thank You for meeting Carol at her place of need today. If necessary Lord, we know You will carry her to her place of healing and give her the miracle she needs. Thank You for being our truly awe-inspiring Heavenly Father. In the Name of Jesus we pray. Amen

Prayer Seventy

Gracious and loving Heavenly Father, we pray in the Name of Jesus, our Lord and Savior. Thank You for planning for us from the beginning and for making us sons and heirs in Your heavenly Kingdom. We are so grateful for Your kindness and love (Ephesians 1:4-6 KJV).

We come before Your Throne once more in the Name of Jesus, asking You to end Carol's suffering. We are lifting her to You with hands of love. We need Your intervention as she remains ill and in pain. She's exhausted, sad and discouraged. We understand her despair. We know this is not what You want for her. *Your plan is for her healing and for her good* (Jeremiah 29:11 *KJV*). Extend Your grace to her now. Reach out Your mighty right arm, and with compassion and love lift her up and pour healing oil to erase each and every symptom she is experiencing. This includes pain, numbness, tingling, burning, blurred vision, sadness, and despair. Speak to her heart with Your sweet words of comfort and send the Holy Spirit and Your angelic hosts to minister to her now.

Thank You for being a faithful God, who has her future well in hand (Lamentations 3:22-23 *KJV*). Amen.

Prayer Seventy-One

King of Kings, Lord of Lords, You are our
wonderful Savior who died for us. We come
to The Father through You and because of
You. You are His exact representation and
are the brilliance of His glory (Hebrews 1: 1-3
KJV). We are so amazed at Your plan and
Your power.

We need delivering power to invade Carol's home, her life and her very cells. We ask You to rest upon her now. Deliver her and heal her. "Lord, Lord God, compassionate and gracious, slow to anger, and abounding in loving kindness and truth" (Exodus 34:6 *KJV*). You are not slow about Your promise, as some count slowness, *but are patient toward us, not wishing for any to perish but for all to come to repentance* (2 Peter 3:9 *KJV*). You are filled with mercy and kindness and we know You will send the very hosts of heaven to fight for her health and well being. *Even when our faith is not enough You remain faithful, You cannot deny Yourself* (2 Timothy 2:13 *KJV*).

Thank You for Your revelation. May Your Word be proclaimed night and day in her household. Heal and deliver Your daughter tonight we pray. Amen.

Prayer Seventy-Two

Abba Father, we come before You in the Name of Jesus. We know You will hear us when we pray (John 14:13-14 KJV).

According to Your Word, "if we have faith the size of a mustard seed we could successfully command a mountain to remove itself to the sea" (Luke 17:6 *NIV*). These are really big promises but we believe them because we do have faith (Matthew 21:21 *KJV*). You mean what You say and say what You mean. We know You are one hundred percent reliable and can be depended upon. That's why we keep right on praying for Carol's healing and deliverance. *You are God and we are not, so You see fully what needs to be done* (Numbers 23:19 *KJV*).

We bind every enemy agent mounting an assault against her and loose peace and tranquility from Your heavenly storehouse (Luke 12:24 *KJV*). *We loose the oil of joy instead of mourning, the garment of praise instead of a disheartened spirit* "She will be called a tree of righteousness, strong and magnificent, distinguished for integrity, justice and right-standing with God. She is a planting of the Lord" (Isaiah 61:3 *AMP*).

She will not be denied the good and perfect gifts You have for her. The assignments of hell are canceled and every effort of the enemy is bound and rendered inactive. "Let Your light break forth like the dawn and her healing quickly appear" (Isaiah 58:8 *AMP*).

Comfort and heal, apply oil and salve to her wounds. Bind her to Your heart and bring deliverance speedily. In the Name of Jesus we thank You for hearing our prayer. Amen.

Prayer Seventy-Three

God of Abraham, Isaac, and Jacob. God of Israel, God of the universe, the ages, and the span of time. We can't imagine how infinite and powerful You are.

Thank You for sending Yeshua to us so we can have an intimate relationship with You. What an honor and privilege. We can only begin to comprehend Your love.

We pray in the Name of Jesus, as we bring our requests, petitions and prayers for Carol to You. Make this day the last day of trials and suffering relating to her health. The devil is totally terrorizing her body and he is trespassing on sacred ground as she is Your daughter. Please rescue her from his arrows, plots, plans, and purposes. *We declare she is under the blood of Jesus and therefore no weapon raised against her can prosper* (Isaiah 54:17 *KJV*). *You are her rock, her shield, her defender, her anchor, her strength, her testimony, her personal bravery, her high tower, her salvation, deliverer and song. Act on her behalf, fight her battles for her and even carry her if necessary.* (Isaiah 46:4 *KJV*).

We proclaim she will live and not die and praise You in this land of the living (Psalm 118:17 *KJV*). Pour out Your healing and favor for her and hear us as we pray. Thank You. Amen.

Prayer Seventy-Four

Abba Father, thank You for answers to prayer. We ask today for faith like Abraham (Romans 3:27:4:25 KJV,) for vision like Elijah (1 Kings 19:11-12 KJV,) courage like Daniel (Daniel 6:10 KJV,) leadership like David (1 Samuel 17:45 KJV,) wisdom like Solomon (1Kings 4:29 KJV,) for strength like Sampson (Judges 15: 13-17 KJV,) and for love like Jesus (John 3:16 KJV).

We want to be equipped to do what You ask of us. Help us we pray.

We proclaim healing, deliverance and freedom for Carol today. We ask for renewal and refreshing of her health and well being. Reverse the damage done to her body, soul and spirit and end this torture the enemy is inflicting upon her. You are the SOVEREIGN of all the universes and all the worlds and have the ability and desire to turn her situation around. We put all our trust and faith in You.

We pray in the victorious name of Yeshua the Messiah. Amen.

Prayer Seventy-Five

Abba Father, thank You for Your grace toward us. Thank You: It is sufficient for today (2 Corinthians 1:12-9 KJV). We know "it is by grace we are saved, not through works, that we should boast" (Ephesians 2:8 NIV). Your grace is freely given and through it we are called Your children.

Today Father we are asking You to extend Your grace to Carol. Let Your grace bring her through this day and this hour. May contemplating Your grace give her hope and strength for today. Remember the calling on her life and grant her healing and shalom. She wants to walk in her destiny but can't do it without Your help. She is weak as a kitten without You, but a roaring lion when You empower her.

You can show Yourself strong in her weakness and all will see Your mighty arm at work (Jeremiah 20:11 *KJV*). Fill her to overflowing with the Holy Spirit. Help her remember that "with You all things are possible and nothing is impossible" (Matthew 19:26 *KJV*). You are more than able to resolve her every problem, to heal and restore her and return to her everything the devil has stolen. We ask You to do that for her. She really needs You to act on her behalf and show her how very much You love her.

Thank You for hearing our prayer and fulfilling our requests. In the Name of Jesus we pray, Amen.

Chapter Eleven

Victory

Consider it nothing but joy, my brothers and sisters, whenever you fall into various trials. Be assured that the testing of your faith (through experience) produces endurance [leading to spiritual maturity and inner peace]. And let endurance have its perfect result and do a thorough work, So that you may be perfect and completely developed [in your faith], lacking in nothing~ (James 1:2-4 AMP).

Prayer Seventy-Six

Precious Jesus, thank You for Your surpassing grace, for Your comfort, and at last for Your victorious right arm! We stand amazed in Your Presence, rejoicing over Your completed work in healing and delivering Carol.

Thank You for opening up Your Word to her, for bringing her family to her bedside, for their prayers, as we knelt and *laid hands on her* (Mark 16:18 *KJV*). We saw her countenance change. We observed as her facial paralysis vanished and her eyes once more followed movement. We saw You, in Your kindness and goodness, clear her head and remove the pain she has endured for more than two decades. We were witnesses to Your amazing love as You cut the chains and freed her from her bed-prison. *We saw the enemy flee* (James 4:7 *KJV*) like a frightened child as You rescued Your daughter from her swamped and sinking ship. You put her feet on God-ground and removed her fears. We saw her family look on in awe as they *watched the deliverance of the Lord* (Exodus 14:13 *KJV*).

We have no words in English or any known language to thank and praise You enough for the glorious power and amazing love we experienced when you answered our prayers for Your daughter and our friend. We extol and adore You for Your loving-kindness towards her and towards us, her prayer team. We rejoice in the Lord our Savior, King of Kings and Lord of Lords. Hallelujah and Amen.

Afterword

It's been a while now since Carol's healing and deliverance and more than two years since my husband was declared cancer free. Both continue to thrive and excel both in health and in service to the King. In the interim, others have used the prayers in this book and seen miraculous results for their loved ones as well. It's possible the words of the prayers matter little, but that the persistence and passion with which they are prayed bring the resulting victories. That's why I encourage you to use the prayers as a template for prayers of your own. Substitute scriptures that hold meaning for you or heart cries that resound with your spirit. The important thing is to pray. Pray! It changes everything.

Remember, it's "out of the fullness of the heart the mouth speaks" (Luke 6:45 *KJV*) or "as a man speaks, so is he" (Matthew 12:34 *KJV*). Learn to pray the Word. When you pray; speak salvation, deliverance, goodness, kindness, self control, freedom, encouraging words, health, and restoration. "Death and life are in the power of the tongue, and those who love it and indulge it will eat its fruit and bear the consequences of their words" (Proverbs 18:21 *KJV*). Jesus tells us just how much our words matter and what an impact they have. Even in prayer we want our words to be operational, full of power and not careless, mechanical, pro forma or hurtful. "But I tell you that every careless word that people speak, they shall give an accounting for it in the Day of Judgment" (Matthew 12:36 *Berean Literal Bible*).

When my husband was going through his chemotherapy and surgery we asked our grandchildren to be part of his healing. We wanted them to feel as if they were part of the outcome. Each time they thought of him or spoke of him we asked them to say "Papa will live!" Now they feel very close to him and know they played a role in his healing and complete recovery. They also know words have power and prayer works.

What are the reasons we feel the need to pray? What usually motivates us to begin praying or take on a prayer assignment? Of course there are many reasons, but most fall into one of these three categories.

1. Habit: we pray because we always say a food blessing or a goodnight prayer. Maybe it's a family tradition or a decision to always honor God in a particular way, but in general we don't give it much thought.

2. Fear: we pray when we are frightened that we are going to lose something or someone or when we feel trapped or desperate. Illness, death, looming change, the unknown, undue stress are all bound to bring us that queasy feeling associated with fear. *It is perfect love and trust in God that removes fear. When we know beyond any shadow of doubt that He will take care of us we can give all our fears to Him* (1 John 4:18 *KJV*).

3. Love: when we have a relationship with God, it's natural to want to talk things over with Him. After all, He knows everything. I love to hang out with Him and I talk to Him about everything. His counsel is unfailingly wise. His precepts are just and true. His wisdom created and maintains all things. He's literally right about everything. He's my life source. Now, I pray first, about everything. My life is so much easier.

> And therefore will the LORD wait, that He may be gracious unto you, and therefore will He be exalted, that He may have mercy upon you: for the LORD is a God of judgment: blessed are all they that wait for Him (Isaiah 30:18 *KJV*).

Still, even when we know we are praying because we have stepped into water over our heads, it can be difficult, and for good reason. For a long time I prayed after everything else failed. Rarely did I race to ask God's help first. Prayer was the last resort. I have learned when prayer is the last resort it means I'm still looking for things to go my way. It's an indicator I still think my solution is probably better than the one God has in store for me. I want what I want, not what He wants. Talking to someone who is invisible can feel pretty weird at first. Believing in something you can't see is counter-intuitive. When He answers, one doesn't usually hear it with their ears, as in a conversation with a friend. Instead we perceive it, or know it from somewhere inside ourselves. How do we know we aren't wasting our time? How do we know our prayers were actually effective in changing a situation or circumstance? According to the Apostle Paul, prayer changes everything. He certainly knew a thing or two about change, seeing that he spread the gospel to the entire civilized world of his day.

Don't allow yourself to be discouraged if the answer seems delayed or you believe yourself not to "be hearing" God's voice. He will answer and you will hear. God will not disappoint you.

Conclusion

In (Ephesians 1:16-21 *AMP*), Paul tells his converts:

> I do not cease to give thanks for you, remembering you in my prayers; I always pray that the God of our Lord Jesus Christ, the Father of glory, may grant you a spirit of wisdom and of revelation [that gives you a deep and personal and intimate insight] into the true knowledge of Him [for we know the Father through the Son]. And I pray that the eyes of your heart [the very center and core of your being] may be enlightened [flooded with light by the Holy Spirit], so that you will know and cherish the hope, the divine guarantee, the confident expectation to which He has called you, the riches of His glorious inheritance in the saints (God's people), and [so that you will begin to know] what the immeasurable and unlimited and surpassing greatness of His [active, spiritual] power is in us who believe. These are in accordance with the working of His mighty strength which He produced in Christ when He raised Him from the dead and seated Him at His

own right hand in the heavenly places, far above all rule and authority and power and dominion [whether angelic or human], and [far above] every name that is named [above every title that can be conferred], not only in this age and world but also in the one to come.

It's in knowing who He is and about His character we can recognize His answers. His answers are always for our good.

Satan hates prayer. He will do anything he can to keep you from praying. He'll steal your time, distract you, try to make you ill, create as much chaos around you as he can. He'll tell you your prayers are inadequate, or stupid, or selfish. He will tell you it's ridiculous to ask for so much. He'll tell you there is no way you are good enough to pray or even that your prayers are outside God's will. *He's the father of lies, remember. There is no truth in him* (John 8:44 *KJV*).

Maybe you are new to prayer or don't know exactly what to say. No problem. Scripture says *both Jesus and the Holy Spirit are interceding for us even now* (Romans 8:24,26 *KJV*). We certainly won't be condemned for learning to pray, we'll be helped.

Have courage to believe you are who God says you are. You are His treasured child and heir. Have the courage to believe that the Word of God is true, that God is real and that you have been on his mind since the foundation of the world. He wants to hear the sound of your voice calling on Him, asking for the desires of your heart.

Pray aloud, pray fervently, pray often. Believe with all your heart.

Your miracle is on its way!

Glossary

Abba	Father
Adonai	Eternal God
Aleph and Tav	Beginning and End, Hebrew
Alpha and Omega	Beginning and End, Greek
Daniel	Biblical man of valor
David	Biblical King of Israel
Elohim	Name of God
El Shaddai	Mighty God
Enemy	The devil
God	God of Israel
Israelites	God's ancient people
Jehova	Name of God
Jehova Saboath	God of the Sabbath
Jehova Rophe	The Lord our Healer
Jesus Christ	Messiah, Son of God
Joshua	Biblical leader of Israelites
Living Word	Jesus
Satan	The devil
Scripture	The Holy Bible
Shalom	Peace
Solomon	Biblical King of Israel
Word of God	Holy Bible
Yeshua	Jesus, Hebrew

Made in the USA
Middletown, DE
20 October 2020